I'M WORKING WHILE THEY'RE SLEEPING

Time Zone Separation Challenges and Solutions

BY ERRAN CARMEL & J. ALBERTO ESPINOSA

Document title: I'M WORKING WHILE THEY'RE SLEEPING
Subtitle: Time Zone Separation Challenges and Solutions
First Edition: November 2011
ISBN: 978-0-9839925-0-9
Version of this book: Print

Published by: Nedder Stream Press
Published in the United States of America

Cover & Book Design: Alison Rayner
Cover image by Cade Martin and Design Army

Trademarks

All brand names and product names referred to in this book are registered trademarks and unregistered trade names of their owners. There is no implied endorsement of any of them.

Disclaimers

This publication aims to provide accurate and reliable information regarding the subject matter covered. However, neither the publisher nor the authors shall be liable for any loss of profit or any other commercial damages, including but not limited to special, incidental, consequential, or other damages.

Visit our website at: **www.timezonecoordination.com**

Table of Contents

Preface

Distance is dead, but time zones are not.

TIME ZONES ARE OFTEN DISCOUNTED or overlooked when companies work globally. We have come to realize that this is actually a new form of global illiteracy because time zone challenges have significant tactical and strategic implications. Time zones are often misunderstood and sloganeered in understanding global collaboration. In fact, we are still surprised when we poll our audiences as we open our talks and ask: "Are time zone differences good or bad?" (What is your answer to this question?) Both experienced and inexperienced audiences are split in their opinions about whether or not time zone differences are advantageous or problematic.

Time zone differences are bad when they lead to inconvenience, delays, and disruptions within an organization. Let's be clear upfront: these types of occurrences affect organizations most of the time. Therefore time zone differences are usually a disadvantage. On the other hand—and much less frequently—time zone separation can be advantageous when work is designed around differences in work shifts using a workflow strategy called "Follow-the-Sun," which merits its own chapter.

Good or bad, organizations need to know how to mitigate time zone challenges because they regularly rely on people scattered around the world. For example, a perfect team might include five smart people: Evgeny in Saint Petersburg, Eitan in Tel Aviv, Nisha in Mumbai, Amanda in Chicago, and Hiro in Kyoto. The team members are not going to gather in, say, Munich tomorrow morning to begin working together. They all have families, and soccer games, and furnished flats. They want to stay where they are—many time zones away from each other. In this book we explain how knowledge workers like Evgeny, Eitan, Nisha, Amanda and Hiro can mitigate the time zone problem and even occasionally leverage time zones.

If you are at the project manager level, mid-level management level, you are likely to feel time zone challenges most acutely. Things can go wrong because of time zone complications in every project. For project managers, the stakes are high for meeting time-to-market, handling complexity, and managing creativity. We therefore submit that mastering time zones can make a difference. We also assert that time zones have not been examined in a holistic manner before. In the well-known Project Management Body of Knowledge (PMBOK), time zones surface implicitly in three of the nine knowledge areas: the "time management" area, especially regarding work sequence; the "communications" area, especially in relation to meetings; and, the "human resource" area. But the PMBOK is silent about the specific challenges and best practices associated with project work across time zones.

WE HAVE ORGANIZED THIS BOOK into three sections. If you cannot read the entire book, then read just the first section, The Fundamentals.

Section I presents the basic information about time zones. In chapter 1 we discuss the time zone problem and some solutions. We also reveal the many folds and layers of time zones. In addition, you will find out if you are "zoner." Chapter 2 is where we compute, diagram, chart, and map time zone differences and time zone configurations. We refer to the collection of time zone diagrams and factors as the "topography" of time zone dispersion. Chapters 3 and 4 are all about solving tactical problems at the project level. "Timeshifting," which we call "the mother of all solutions," is covered extensively from all angles in chapter 3, and in chapter 4 we discuss the mélange of other time zone solutions, tools and processes, including technologies.

Section II is about strategy. Time zones and strategy have never been fused together elsewhere. No one has written about time zones from a strategic perspective. In chapter 5 we begin with location—at least the temporal one: time zone position matters. Decision makers need to pay attention to time zones when designing their distributed organization. This brings us to chapter 6 where we explore the misunderstood strategies of Follow-the-Sun and Round-the-Clock. Both these approaches leverage time zone separation, but for very different purposes. Follow-the-Sun is about speed and calendar efficiencies. Round-the-Clock is about 24-hour coverage. We outline some radical strategies that can be used and practiced in chapter 7. We consider them radical because, first of all, they are relatively new and, second, because these two strategies involve creating a culture that is focused on time zone differences. The first strategy implements a 24-hour organizational culture; the second strategy time-shifts everyone to full overlap and then simulates co-location.

Section III is titled "Time and a Half" because we include extra time-related topics. Chapter 8 is about health and wellness when working across time zones. Given that time zone separation demands timeshifting into evenings or nights, sometimes over long periods, we cover medical and social well-being, the biology of circadian rhythms, as well as labor regulations. Perceptions about time are examined in chapter 9. After all, humans' time perspectives are, without question, highly subjective. Each individual has different time visions, and a person's group, gender, culture, and societal rhythms influences such visions. And since time separation introduces periods of quiet, we also take a look at the sub-discipline of interruption science. Finally, in chapter 10 we bring in some theory, inspired by Lewin's adage that there is nothing more practical than a good theory. We've written this chapter for non-academic readers who are interested in learning what coordination theory can teach us about mitigating the time zone problem.

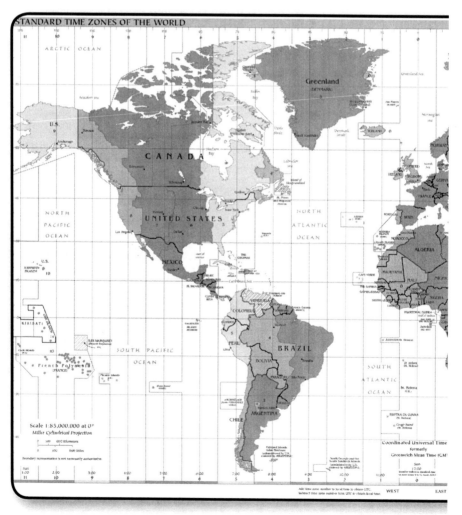

Prologue:
The Story of Time Zones

At noon on November 18, 1883, the trains on the Louisville & Nashville Railroad line in the southeastern United States deliberately remained at a standstill for eighteen minutes. There was nothing wrong with the trains. Rather, the trains were transitioning to the correct time zone. This was the day that the United States standardized to four time zones. On that day,

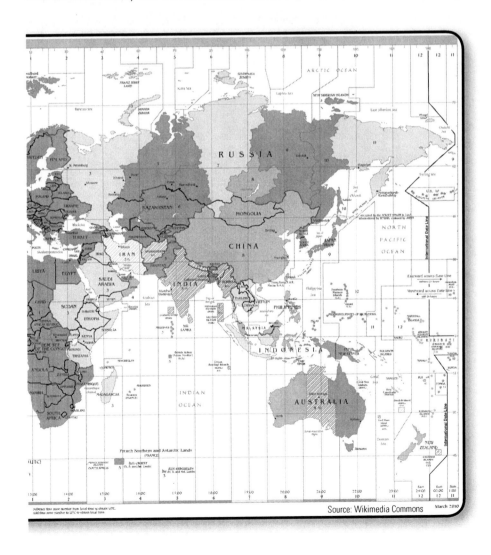

Source: Wikimedia Commons   March 2010

the new, correct time was disseminated by telegraph to post offices, government offices and railway stations across the country. From this point on, it was believed that all activities would be synchronized.

OUR STORY OF TIME ZONES is about society's quest for synchronization—a long journey that began even before that auspicious day in 1883. Synchronization began with the calendar—humankind's first major invention to establish temporal regularity. The calendar is primarily responsible for the creation of those regular patterns through which nearly all societies, social institutions and social groups introduce some order into their lives.[1] After the calendar came the clocks. The first "clock," the sundial, was in existence well before biblical times. Mechanical clocks followed in the 13th century, and in the 19th century, clocks were miniaturized into watches.

However, all these time-telling devices can only sync to their local times. They do not tell the time in another town or on the other side of the world. People gradually recognized the shortcomings of the device. As travel became increasingly faster, they understood the importance of discovering a way to coordinate time between longer distances. All these circumstances lead to the core of our story—time zones.

A Brief History of Time Zones

IN 18TH CENTURY ENGLAND there was little communication between cities, towns or villages. Each settlement kept its own time and lived in its own time zone aided by its own church bell. England was a small country without much variation in longitude, so the discrepancy between towns may have only been about twenty minutes.

The discrepancies were unremarkable until 1784, when the British mail coach service started to run according to fixed schedules. Coach drivers needed to move their own clocks as they traveled from town to town. It became clear that time coordination between post offices would make operations much smoother.[2]

By the early 1800s, trains began running in England. Scheduling problems became more acute with the introduction of this new mode of transportation, so train schedules were synchronized to London Time (during those days, what we now call Greenwich Time was called London Time). By 1855, the need for time synchronization forced most towns in Britain to observe the same clock. In the United States, similar problems and solutions emerged as the railroad system grew rapidly across the much larger nation. Before standardization, there were often two clocks at American railroad stations—one showing local time, which was governed by the sun, and the other showing railroad time, which was governed by the railroad line. If more than one railroad line came through the city, then more clocks were needed. Usually, the times were not very far apart.

New technologies, such as mail coaches, trains and telegraph, were all part of the growing wad of hassles that coaxed the development of time synchronization. In 1869, an American named Charles Dowd put forth the notion of national time zones for the United States. He conceived of four time zones for the United States, separated by fifteen degrees. Fourteen years later, on November 18, 1883, the United States standardized to four time zones and train scheduling became less complex.

But the use of time zones was not yet global. Today's image of the globe, nicely wrapped with time zone bands, was not yet in place. The concept of global time zones was first proposed by Sandford Fleming, a Canadian railroad engineer, in 1876. His proposal led to the international Meridian conference of 1884 during which the Greenwich meridian, over many political disagreements, was agreed to be the world's only meridian. With the earth's time center established, the technocrats could now draw twenty-four time zones around the world, separated by exactly one hour.

Today, time standardization across time zones is officially referred to as Universal Time, abbreviated as UTC, where the C refers to "coordinated." Since this is the same time convention as the traditional name, Greenwich Mean Time (GMT), the GMT is still commonly used and we'll use it in this book. **We will be explicit about these notations since this is a book about time and time zones. All times will be expressed using the 24-hour format: midnight is 00:00; 11 a.m. is 11:00; and, 5:45 p.m. is 17:45. Time zone location is expressed in GMT: Washington, D.C., home of the authors of this book, is UTC/GMT -5 hours, or just GMT -5 for short.**

- **Russia** once spanned 11 time zones, including isolated Kaliningrad on the Baltic Sea. But Russia went on a time zone diet in 2010, moving far away Kamchatka 1 time zone closer to Moscow, and eliminating one other small time zone. Russia now spans **10** time zones.
- **Canada** spans **6** time zones.
- The **United States** spans **4** time zones on the main part of the continent, but Hawaii is 2 time zones west of California, effectively meaning that the United States spans 6 time zones.
- **Brazil** spans **3** time zones, though nearly all its population is in the Eastern time zone (GMT -3). If the tiny Fernando de Noronha islands are included, as some Brazilians insist, then Brazil spans 4 time zones.
- **Australia** spans **3** time zones. However, note that its central states use the half hour. In addition, one small strip of Western Australia has its own unofficial time zone.
- **Mexico** spans **3** time zones, though nearly all its industry is in GMT -6.
- **China** has only **1** time zone, GMT +8. It is the world's widest-spanning time zone. Before the revolution of 1949, China was separated into 5 time zones.
- **India** has had only **1** time zone, GMT +5:30, since its independence. Notice the half hour. Repeated attempts to add time zones in this large country have been unsuccessful.

Why Not Abolish Time Zones?

WHILE TIME ZONES ARE NOW well established, it would be quite convenient if everybody used exactly the same time regardless of where they were on Earth. No one would have to adjust his or her clock. No one would have to ask: "How many time zones away are you?" Wouldn't it be nice if time zones were abolished?

Two groups of professionals who work across many time zones, international pilots and the American military, adjusted to this idea of one standard global time. Pilots tend to use GMT, while the U.S. military calls its standard global time Zulu. All time is denominated in GMT/Zulu regardless of where the person or event is located. Similarly, computer-based group calendars such as Microsoft Outlook uses standard time, GMT, as the basis for adjusting and computing time differences.

In a similar vein, at the dawn of the Internet Age, a radical initiative was proposed to address the new realities of global coordination:[3] not only would the bothersome time zones be abolished, but humanity would take the opportunity to reengineer the archaic way we measure time. In 1998, the watch company Swatch introduced a new time standard called "Internet Time," a time zone free standard. Every location on the globe would have exactly the same time, which would make global coordination much simpler. Time would be measured in "beats," with 1000 beats per day (a beat is about 1.5 of today's minutes). Mid-day would be represented as @500, and would occur at the same moment all over the world. In Internet Time, @500 is noon in Switzerland (home of Swatch), late afternoon in India, and time to go to sleep in Sydney. But, Internet Time was treated as a lark. The rise of the Internet was not impetus enough to discard the measures of time that were so deeply etched into our daily existence.

Time zones are profoundly useful. All literate people "know" that people go to work around 08:00, have lunch at around 12:00, head back home around 18:00, and go to sleep around 23:00. All that is needed is the time zone offset to figure out where to find someone. With Internet Time, humankind would not have to worry about time conversions. But how do you figure out when someone on the other side of the globe is having lunch? In sum, regardless of the time synchronization method, time separation issues will endure!

SECTION I
The Fundamentals

The four chapters of this section present the necessary background and usable knowledge to understand work coordination across time zones.

Chapter 1 presents the many facets of the time difference challenge—it goes beyond time zones, as you will see—and begins to offer solutions.

Chapter 2, the "topography" of time zone dispersion, is where we compute, diagram, chart, and map time zone differences and time zone configurations.

Chapters 3 and 4 are all about solving tactical problems at the project level. In chapter 3 we discuss timeshifting, which is the adjustment of one's work hours and is "the mother of all solutions."

In Chapter 4, we present the mélange of other time zone solutions, tools and processes, including technologies.

CHAPTER 1

Introduction

Introduction

It is 09:30 India Standard Time, and Kuldeep, a software engineer in information technology (IT) production support is frustrated. He cannot re-create the software defect based on what was logged into the issue/defect system during the night. He has no one to call. The author of the defect report, an American who lives and works 10.5 time zones away, is now sleeping. So the Indian software engineer resorts to writing a lengthy e-mail requesting clarification. Solving the problem is delayed by one day... at the very least.

THE COORDINATION BREAKDOWN represented in this vignette stems from time zone separation. There are countless others like it in many knowledge professions. While such coordination breakdowns are common today, these time zone challenges are relatively new. Until the 1980s, time zone separation did not matter much. Sure it mattered for airline pilots and ministers of foreign affairs, but for the vast majority of knowledge workers, it had little impact on daily work. Then, in the 1980s, the fax machine became a ubiquitous form of communication. This made it possible for some work objects—documents, designs, accounts and programs—to be transferred instantly across time zones.

Still, even into the mid-1990s, geographic distance was more important than time zone differences because shipping a work object took days and cost a lot of money. In that ancient era, software professionals air-shipped floppy disks and magnetic tape reels inscribed with computer code. Coordination between distant collaborating sites was, at best, what we could call *loosely coupled*. Yes, the sites were interdependent, but not much.

Then the Internet came along and, all of a sudden, time zone differences mattered.

Today, shipping digital goods is almost free and essentially instantaneous. Indeed, distance is essentially dead, but time differences have become the principal obstacle to efficient coordination. This is because differences in time zones are more difficult to overcome than distance separation. As task times become more compressed and time pressures increase to meet market demands,

> **Coordination is the act of integrating each task and organizational unit so that it contributes to the overall objective.**

coordination across time zones becomes the elephantine problem hidden in plain view.

Coordination across many time zones is a problem *inherently hard to solve* without some radical measures because human beings need to sleep. For example, all locations could be forced to shift their work hours to achieve 100 percent work time overlap, thus solving, at least technically, the time zone problem. But humans tend to work during daylight hours due to deeply embedded biological and societal norms. Humans and all biological organisms have circadian rhythms that synchronize with the light and dark cycles of the day. They cannot live without sleep, nor can they break their circadian rhythms. Scientists have tried, but in the short-term future, these are the laws of nature, and we suggest accepting them as such.

Indeed, once the number of time zones between collaborators is larger than about nine hours, the time zone gap becomes a chasm. While one designer is working, the other designer, with whom coordination is needed, is away or asleep. Fancy videoconferencing cannot overcome this fundamental problem, no matter how high the pixel density and no matter how small the video latency. The time zone problem can be mitigated, as we will review in great detail, but it cannot be eradicated. For example, if programmers in Bangalore (India, GMT +5:30) and Boston (United States, GMT-5) collaborate, they may timeshift somewhat to create some work time overlap, but the time zone problem will be exacerbated when collaborating programmers are added in Silicon Valley (United States, GMT-8).

The ripples of large time differences are very real: from the operational, to the political. When we visited Yahoo's software research and development (R&D) center in remote Trondheim, Norway, north of the Arctic Circle, we learned that time zones were the single biggest problem in distributed work. The Yahoo headquarters in California was nine time zones away, so there was no natural overlap time. It was difficult to communicate, let alone exert influence on decision-making. Delays were common. All senior managers in Norway were quite troubled by the time zone difference.

There is no denying that these time zone coordination problems may seem rather mundane, even banal, when one breaks them down into a workflow. For example, two experienced collaborators working across time zones may rely heavily on e-mail. These e-mail messages become requests for clarification in the form of: "Can you explain or clarify this for me, please?" Without clarification, one side is stuck waiting. Worse, in many cases, the first clarification is insufficient. Meanwhile, several days go by. In fact, our research in this area has shown that *delay* is at the heart of the difficulty organizations experience when trying to coordinate work across time zones.

Delay is the first and most important category of the direct time zone *costs*: the costs of coordinating some sort of work object (e.g., a document, a program, or an action). Delay is one of three components of these time zone coordination costs along with the costs of rework and switching costs. Delay costs are the costs incurred because one site is waiting for another to begin the workday. Rework costs, which come about due to time zone induced miscommunication when one site makes errors that later need to be fixed, generally lead to even further delay. Finally, switching costs are the costs of restarting a task due to waiting.

But these rational cost components don't even begin to take into account the frustrating, time-wasting, common mistakes made in coordinating meetings across time zones, such as missing the meeting by one hour because of time zone computation error. Even seasoned globe-trotters make these mistakes. Nor do these costs take into account the time zone reverberations that disrupt work rhythms. Our research, and that of others such as John Tang of Microsoft Research, finds that time zone differences alter the rhythm of workflow, and the sense of time is disrupted in distributed time-separated groups.

Some years ago we wrote: "All things being equal, any manager would prefer to manage a co-located team rather than a distributed team."[4] This is still true today because of the advantages of co-location. In spite of better technology, humans working in close proximity can act more quickly to sync with each other: They can *transmit* the needed information to each other and *converge* on ideas, tasks, and problems.[5]

Yet, even with these time zone challenges, global firms have all plunged dramatically into dispersed work. For example, by 2003 Intel was already an extremely virtual company. An internal study at the time[6] showed that on a weekly basis, Intel was conducting 8,300 web-based collaborations and 19,000 audio bridges. Seventy one percent of employees collaborated with people who spoke other languages. Almost two-thirds of Intel employees were multi-teaming (acting as members on more than three teams). By 2007, 40% of IBM employees worked remotely, and 70% of IBM managers supervised at least one remote worker.[7] Infosys, a major Indian offshore outsourcing firm, routinized its work across time zones with an approach it labeled "Global Delivery Model," designed to guide work coordination between the Indian IT engineers and its faraway American clients.

Beyond software, most industries have now moved to "global product development," which is just another euphemism for distributed work. Boeing's 787 Dreamliner had 1,000 suppliers in dozens of global locations. Lockheed Martin's F-35 jet fighter had work teams in nine partner countries on four continents, and the project shared "design packages" daily around its sites. To summarize these many vignettes of the business landscape: More people are dependent every day on others who are many time zones away.

Of course, time zone differences are not the only challenge to distributed global collaborations. There are many barriers and, when they align, they create "fault lines" in distributed collaboration which are very difficult to bridge. There are differences in culture, language, organizational approaches, technology infrastructure, and even business process differences. For example, in one global company we visited there were differences in how to request paper to re-fill the printers. The Americans could not understand why it took so long to print documents in India until, after much frustration, they learned about the tedious paperwork required to procure a ream of paper at the Indian outsourcing firm.

From the petty to the profound, all these fault lines bring about significant, serious problems that cause many global collaborators to tear their hair out. We, along with other authors, have been writing about these challenges since the 1990s. However, in this book we focus deliberately *only* on the time zone differences, while setting aside other fault lines.

Time Zones and Why
The Time Zone Map Is Hard To Use

THE FAMILIAR TIME ZONE WORLD MAP is a common backdrop these days, conveying worldliness, connectedness, and the magnificence of the networked globe. While all nations now adhere to standard time zones, there are several factors that increase time zone complexity for all who coordinate across them. As a result of these complications, the time zone world map is a nice piece of modern artwork, but is nearly unusable because the vertical time zone lines are so inconsistent. Most have been established by politics, not by science.

Foremost is the uneven practice of Daylight Saving Time (DST). DST was first practiced in Germany during World War I. Now, a century later, it is practiced in some but not all locations. Moreover, some countries change the DST start and end dates somewhat erratically (e.g., Israel); some national regions have their own DST policy (e.g., the state of Arizona in the United States); and some smaller areas have DST policies, such as the Navajo Nation in northeastern Arizona which observes DST even when the rest of the state does not. Separately, most countries around the equator do not use DST since the seasonal difference in sunlight is minimal. Regrettably, DST changes often lead to synchronization problems in the various e-calendars that govern most everyone's lives.

The second complicating factor is the gradual westernization of time zone boundaries in order to have more daylight late in the day. The fashion is to push time zone boundaries west of their designated meridians. For example, the Spanish city of La Coruña on the Atlantic observes Central European time (GMT +1). In summer, with the added boost of DST, the sun sets in La Coruña after 22:00, making it feel almost Nordic.

The third complicating factor is that some nations can't settle on nice round numbers. Some countries and regions do not use the suggested one-hour increment from zone to zone, but rather one half hour. India is the most famous case (GMT +5:30), followed by Newfoundland and Venezuela. Nepal even uses quarter-hour deviation (GMT +5:45).

The large nations seem to be on time zone diets in quest of simplification. China uses a *single* time zone with no DST (GMT +8). It is the country with the widest time zone in the world. In 1949, Mao's Communist revolution abolished China's five time zones and replaced them with one time zone. Politics has also changed the Russian time zones. As every Russian has known for generations, the country is so vast that it spans eleven time zones. No longer. In 2010, Russian President Medvedev announced some time zone reengineering, effectively reducing the Russian vastness down to only a span of ten time zones.

Beyond Time Zones: National Holidays and Other Calendar Differences That Hinder Coordination

AS WE DISCOVERED WHEN WE BEGAN to study coordination across time differences, time zones are not the only time inhibitors to global coordination. There are calendar differences. Try scheduling an inter-team voice conference several months into the calendar year. You may find that your Canadian team is away for a "late" Easter, then the Dutch team is away for Queen's Day, followed by the Russian team celebrating the two-week May Day spring holiday, and, finally, the Hong Kong team takes a day's leave because of Buddha's Birthday. The number of days in the year in which there is no national holiday at any site within a large global firm is remarkably small. Typically only about a quarter of a year's workdays are available across *all* global sites for meetings, videoconferences, or company retreats.

Specifically, there are *six* calendar differences that complicate global coordination. They all complicate global coordination. The differences are expressed by these irritated comments: "I cannot understand their work hours," and continue with: "I'm working while they're at (a long) lunch," or "They've left for the weekend," or the very popular "They always seem to be on a holiday."

Work hours and number of hours per week. Daily work hours vary by country. For example, American traditional hours are 09:00-17:30, or more colloquially, "9 to 5," in a forty-hour workweek. For many years, workers in France were only allowed by law to work thirty-five hours per week. In India, formal work hours for technology firms are from 09:30 to 18:00. In China, traditional work hours are from 08:00 to 18:00, with a two-hour lunch break. Huawei, China's most successful technology company, has kept the two-hour lunch tradition, but most other technology firms moved to 09:00-18:00 with the international one-hour lunch break. Americans are more likely to plunge into work as soon as they get to the office, while the French, who tend to begin the workday later than Americans, tend to spend the first period of their office time in small talk with co-workers.

Lunchtime. Lunch breaks turn out to be major disruptors of overlap windows. We are amazed at how often we hear gripes about this topic. Here are two instances. A Portugal-based manager (GMT + 0) said about his Brazilian partners (GMT −3): "When we arrive, they are sleeping. When we go for lunch, they arrive. When we come back from lunch, we have four hour overlap, if not less." In Europe, German and British collaborators discovered, to their consternation, that even their one-hour time zone difference substantially affected the team's ability to overlap. Total overlap time was reduced by three hours: one hour at the edge of the day and two hours during each site's lunch break.

Therefore, it is useful to consider the norms of lunch breaks, which are different in each nation and region. Americans break for lunch rather obsessively between 12:00-13:00, and tend to avoid breaking later. Europeans will take their lunch break later and, in places such as Spain, may have long lunch breaks. In some places everyone goes to lunch together, less so in the United States. Some organizations have acculturated the unsocial habit of eating lunch at one's desk. In some Muslim nations, Friday lunch break is two hours to allow for prayer.

Weekends. Most of the world has moved to a two-day weekend of Saturday-Sunday, but this is an on-going process.[8] Hong Kong had a 5.5-day workweek until recently—and such a workweek can still be found in some Latin American countries. The choice of Saturday-Sunday is anchored on the Christian Sabbath of Sunday. This has created a synchronization problem with the Jewish and Muslim Sabbath—Friday sundown through Saturday sundown and Friday, respectively. Jewish Israel and some Muslim nations practice weekends of Friday-Saturday, which means four workdays overlap with most of the world. At the same time, some Muslim nations have gone further, choosing Thursday-Friday as their weekend, which means only three workdays overlap, and in Palestine's two regions there are two different weekends.[9]

Holidays. When is the best time to schedule a global voice conference? Michael Segalla[10] looked at twelve major global cities and found that taking holidays out of the mix eliminated 25% of workdays in 2011. Even more remarkable, he found that only fifteen of a year's workweeks (29%) were uninterrupted by a holiday. Alas, these are easy to discover, since holiday schedules can be easily found on Internet calendars, but the *hidden* holiday work slowdowns are not documented. For example, Americans do minimal work in the ten days before Christmas; Muslims get less work done during the Ramadan month of fasting.

Vacations. Americans have, on average, about twelve days of annual vacation leave and take a few days at a time. The Dutch have thirty-two days per year and take long vacations. The French take long summer vacations, and almost no one works during the month of August in Spain.

Equatorial. Most global knowledge workers live north of the equator and take summer holidays from June through August. South Africans and Australians, of course, don't do that. Vacation schedules become disruptive in North–South collaborations. Referring to his Brazilian counterparts, a Portuguese manager said that, "When we want to go full speed ahead in January after the Christmas holiday, then Brazil is on their summer vacation. When we are moving slowly in July/August, Brazil wants to move fast."

The portrayal of these six calendar differences shouldn't be seen as entirely bleak. While they do make collaboration more chaotic, managers do have the power to reduce some of these time differences. For example, we heard a Sri Lankan technocrat lament about managing call centers out of Sri Lanka. He said, "We have twenty-six public holidays. There is one holiday for every full moon. We celebrate Christian, Hindu and Muslim holidays. If a holiday is on Thursday, people take Friday off." Naturally, one cannot run an export-oriented, globally connected industry around that kind of calendar. The technocrat continued to explain, "However, in export zones, we have been released from national labor laws. It is an enclave. Workers are paid much more than elsewhere so they are happy without the [full menu of holidays]."

With all their wrinkles, time differences are the rational, predictable part of the global collaboration workday. The other part, explained next, is fuzzier and evolving. It is the bedrock, the structure of work.

The Changing Structure of Work

Very few of the world's knowledge workers are working as their parents did. Much of this change is due to advances in technology, but another part is due to a change in norms. Thus we look at the backdrop for collaboration across time zones: from 24/7 to "Scattertime."

Speed, workweeks, and workdays

Speed is one of the drivers of the new culture of work: fast food, fast service, fast cycle and fast response. Global workers are time-sensitive, deadline-driven and impatient. Digital workers expect an immediate response to e-mail. Now! Lines need to be short. Waiting times have to be reduced to seconds. Jack Welch, former CEO of GE and a big business guru, famously asserted that, "Speed is everything." Products have to be developed faster and faster. This is known as *hyper competition*. Cars took seven years to develop in the 1970s, three years in the 1980s, two years by the 2000s. Mortgage loan applications, which used to take months to process, now only take a few days. Today, the wildest hyper-competitive segment is the mobile/smart phones, including the handset and its software and services. For all the talk of flexibility, there is no respite from the spiral of speed. If one can do something fast, an even faster way is expected.[11]

Speed cannot be achieved within traditional conventions of work so all economies are witnessing the disappearance of the traditional, regimented, five-day, approximately forty-hour workweek. Historically, this structure has only been found in wealthy nations for about a century. In the 20th century, as societies moved away from the farm to the city and became wealthier, the number of work hours decreased and became normatively fixed. Weekends became common off the farm.

The decline of the traditional workweek structure was predicted and written about by the famous futurist Alvin Toffler in his 1980 book, "The Third Wave." The traditional workweek span is from 06:00 to 18:00 Monday through Friday. Today, only 24% of Europeans work solely within this span. Conversely, in both the United States and the European Union, approximately

17% of the workforce works completely outside this traditional span.[12] And the large remaining portion of workers overlaps traditional hours in various ways.

The traditional workweek is giving way to a 24-hour business culture. Originally, this was an American innovation that began with 24-hour petrol stations, food-markets and all-night restaurants. Earlier in the century, factory workers were assigned shift work in factories that sometimes operated twenty-four hours a day using three shifts of workers. During the postwar era in Europe, there was a reluctance to move to the hyper-speed that was associated with America. It has been only in recent years that Germans, for example, have moved to extended store hours, with some even open twenty-four hours.

The label "24/7" conveys cool and hip. And consumers expect 24/7. We first exercised in a 24-hour gym back in 1984 and pondered: "Why does anybody need a 24-hour gym?" Later, in Silicon Valley, the puzzle was solved for us. Some of those who exercised were the high-tech workers who woke up at mad hours for global conference calls and then drove to the gym after the call was over.

"I'll Sleep When I'm Dead," is a mantra that can be found in the titles of songs, movies, and even a coffee chain campaign. After all, sleep is a waste. Humans spend about a third of their lives just sleeping or preparing for sleep. It is likely that before the end of this century there will be drugs that will allow for round-the-clock living. The first small steps have already been taken. For example, during the 2003 invasion of Iraq, British and American troops used Modafinil to keep themselves going without sleep.

Notwithstanding the hipness of 24/7, overtime work is the other contributor to the demise of the traditional workweek. In the United States, workweeks of fifty to sixty hours for knowledge workers have been common for decades. Japan in the postwar era was notorious for its long hours for the "salary man," the white-collar worker staying late in his Tokyo office tower. During this same era, Europeans lagged behind the Japanese and Americans in the length of workweeks, but work hours in Europe have increased in recent years. Rankings from a study conducted by UBS[13] compiled the average number of hours worked per year in major cities. The top cities, Abu Dhabi, Bogotá, Hong Kong, Taipei, Manila and a few more were over 2,100 hours per year; Los Angeles was 1,939; Berlin at 1,616; and Paris was only 1,587. This means that Parisians work roughly 25% fewer hours than those in the emerging economies at the top of the list.

Scattertime – the scattered workday

Scattertime – the fragmented, splintered day, mixing work and non-work activities.
Nomadism – working anyplace. Many nomads work in cafés, in "third places," not their home or office.

Scattertime is the relatively new mode of work, often driven by global time zone differences. We coined this term to describe the work structures we have been observing in the last decade. Knowledge workers spread out their labor into chunks of time interrupted by childcare, exercise, shopping, leisure, nap, social networking, family dinner, or sleep. It's all interspersed, intermingled. It's scattered. Also important for our topic, scattertime implies that each worker is, essentially, in his/her own time zone. In the United States, about 35% of technology workers have some flexibility in their work hours and are able to vary their work hours to some degree.[14]

Scattertime has other names[15] such as "flexible work style" and "flexi-time." Sun Microsystems called it "open work." Meanwhile, nomadism[16] may displace the dated thinking about telecommuting, which assumes one works from home. Nomadism and scattertime are nicely orthogonal—nomadism describes the concept of place while scattertime describes time.

Related to scattertime is "anytime, anywhere," which has become one of the clichés of our era. Advertisements try to make this concept desirable by portraying an attractive office worker sitting on an *uncrowded* beach with a laptop. The slogan should more accurately be "all the time, everywhere." With new technology gadgets, knowledge workers can work at home, in the car, and on vacation, making a 24-hour workday possible. The train and the airplane used to serve as a place to relax and to read a book, but now serve as a mobile office.

In a sense, scattertime represents the pendulum swinging back to pre-industrial times. Back then home and work were co-located on the farm or in the village. Since the industrial era, home and work have been separated because work requires people and assets to be physically together. Thus the traditional notion of work has been shaped by a clear dividing line between "work time," which is "owned" by the employer, and "leisure time," which is "owned" by the individual. Now knowledge workers are returning to having home and work together. And the younger generation of workers, already digital natives, are used to fiddling with their gadgets on nights and weekends.

Yet, there are positive aspects to scattertime because it allows individuals some control in planning their workday according to their priorities, such as a tennis game or childcare.

However, this sense of control is not evenly distributed in the population. Dutch researchers[17] conducted a study of "9-to-5" to see the effects of individuals' control over their own schedules. They even gave this control an elegant label, "time sovereignty." The researchers found that control over working time is determined more by education level than by working atypical hours.

Control over work time is a continuum and is, ultimately, quite subjective. Now that knowledge workers have gadgets, should they let work permeate every segment of their day? This is the dilemma of work-life balance. Hence, scattertime may well come at a cost. Knowledge workers live with expectations of quick response during non-traditional hours. If the boss sends an e-mail message at 23:00, does she expect a reply that night? One American programmer told us that he turns off the awareness button when he logs on in the evening so that his Chinese colleagues will not be tempted to ask him questions as they come into work in the morning. What about Sundays? While some American knowledge workers work on Sundays on occasion, we heard from one who complained that he was being treated differently because he "doesn't do Sundays" since he's a churchgoer. All global workers have their own boundaries. We devote chapter 8 to the health, stress, and the social costs of speed, overtime, and scattertime that come from working across time zones.

Zoners

THERE ARE MANY TIME ZONE natives these days. These are the globalized workers who are comfortable moving across time zones. We call them *zoners*. Every book needs a hero and zoners are the heroes of this book.

Zoners have a deeply ingrained sense of temporal distance and its implications. We see this as somewhat analogous to the continuum of people's spatial ability: There are those who can read maps and take directions well and those who cannot (and who always seem to get lost). We think zoners are "born" with some of their abilities, but these, of course, get refined with experience.

Zoners are less likely to get confused with time zone computations, while others can never seem to remember how many time zones away, say, California happens to be, and will frequently miss meetings because of a time-zone misunderstanding. Zoners are able to keep in mind the perennial problem of time zone differences. They use timeanddate.com, everytimezone.com, and worldtimebuddy.com and know how to adjust the time zone on their Outlook calendars and smartphones. They pack their bags with melatonin and when they wake up in a strange place, they always know what time it is. Zoners are also good sleepers since their life involves a good amount of timeshifting.

Zoners also know the special tricks of multi-time zone work. For example, one important trick is to tackle time zone induced delays by *breaking the e-mail chain*. The e-mail chain begins when, in time-separated asynchronous communication, the sender initiates a message, and the receiver, on the other side of the globe, does not understand it fully and asks for clarification. The original sender attempts to clarify, but the receiver is unable to interpret the clarification and sends another request for clarification. Meanwhile, an entire week has passed. Zoners stop this chain early by picking up the phone to clarify the message and move the task along.

The Two Most Common Time Zone Management Questions

WE WRAP UP THIS FIRST CHAPTER by addressing two of the most common time zone questions head on: "When is the best time to meet?" and "What is the optimal time zone difference?"

When do I meet? Figuring out when to schedule a meeting across time zones

Even when all individuals are in the same location, figuring out when to meet is a very frustrating task. It is even more so when team members are widely scattered across time zones. One often hears how draining it is to schedule a multi-time zone meeting. So we recommend setting up a rhythm of regularly scheduled meetings, since these will need to be negotiated and scheduled just once. The market now provides a myriad of scheduling and calendar tools[18] (see Appendix A). IBM has a slick tool on the company's internal website called "time zone pain" that tries to minimize the collective pain of finding a time window that is the least disruptive. A similar popular tool is called "meeting planner," freely available on timeanddate.com. Setting regular meetings also reduces the perennial time zone mistake: "Oops, I thought you were three hours away, not four." or "Oops, sorry for waking you up; I thought you were three hours ahead, not three hours behind."

And what if the group is extremely far-flung? The meeting planning software cannot perform miracles. What is the best time to meet then? In some organizations, the powerful choose the timeslot that is convenient for them so they will not be inconvenienced.[19] But we will ignore that as the correct answer. The correct answer is either Mumbai time or rotating time. Let's start with Mumbai. Michael Segalla[20] provocatively stated that: "Mumbai at 13:00 is the center of the business world." Lunchtime in Mumbai, or any Indian city, spans the workday of East Asia, Australia, the Persian Gulf, South Africa, and much of Europe. It is the United States that is actually isolated time zone-wise. The American workday overlaps with very little of the workday of those in the Eastern Hemisphere. To recap, by default, schedule your meeting at 13:00 IST (GMT +5.5).

Then again, just as soon as the meeting leader schedules a meeting across time zones, someone is inconvenienced. The colleague who regularly falls asleep during global conference calls may be a familiar character to some readers. A partial remedy to the time zone pain is to share the pain by regularly *rotating* the timeslots so that the same people are not inconvenienced all the time. We find rotation in many companies we visit, including Intel (see chapter 4) and Microsoft.[21] It is a reasonable, democratic tactic.

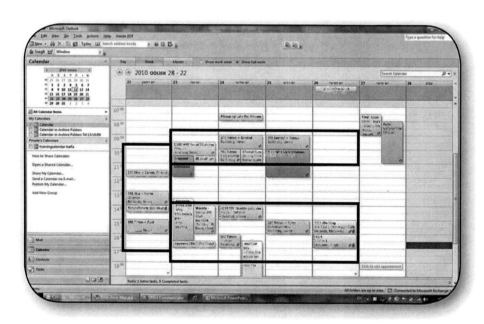

Figure 1-1: Weekly calendar planning influenced by time zones.
This example is of a "C" shaped meeting schedule from an Israel-based organization as viewed in a Microsoft Outlook calendar. The C is evident in the rectangles drawn around blocks of meeting time and date entries.

When to meet is a topic that also impacts that other temporal device—calendar planning. Organizations should design their calendars around time zone differences. A nice illustration of the intersection of time zones and calendars comes from an Israeli zoner, Yaron Berlinsky of Philips, the giant Dutch corporation. Yaron regularly schedules meetings around the world. He introduced us to the Israeli "C" of calendar planning based on his project's time differences (fig. 1-1). The left side of the C is so formed because Israelis work on Sundays (since the weekend is Friday-Saturday). An effective use of time is to schedule meetings between the local Israeli team members on Sundays. The top of the C is formed from the meetings with the Bangalore (India) unit, which are scheduled Monday through Thursday mornings (08:00 – 11:00 Israel time, 11:30 – 14:30 India Standard Time). Meetings with those on the East Coast of the United States form the bottom of the C as they are scheduled Monday through Thursday afternoons (14:00 – 17:00 Israel time, 07:00 – 10:00 EST).

What is the optimal time zone difference?

Zero! Usually. For most types of work, for most organizations, for most teams, the answer is zero.[22] Overall, there is now some empirical evidence that shows degradation as time difference increases and furthermore, there is empirical evidence that shows degradation when the sites have no overlap. Two of these are our own studies. In our own laboratory experiment on time zones with our colleague Ning Nan we found that there is some degradation of quality as the time zone differences grow.[23] With our colleagues Jonathon Cummings and Cindy Pickering, we found that at Intel, once dyads of individuals cross the threshold into no time overlap, this increases delay.[24] McKinsey consultants Siebdrat and colleagues also found that performance generally degrades with time zone separation. Their data are summarized in figure 1-2.

A more nuanced answer to the question of optimal time separation largely depends on the task and the architecture of the task. Undoubtedly, as we describe in chapter 6, time zone differences can be an advantage in some cases, but this leads us to the corollary: When the time zone differences are large, the organization works differently. The workflows between collaborators, teams, professionals, stakeholders, and companies can change, sometimes dramatically, depending on time zone differences.

And now for the caveat: we often hear the claim that a small amount of time zone difference may be beneficial. While working in the same time zone provides the widest window for same-time interaction, it also leads to more interruptions. Having a small time difference may spur the team to establish more synchronized workflow practices with some quiet time for individual work. After all, when the team is busy coordinating, the actual task is not getting done.

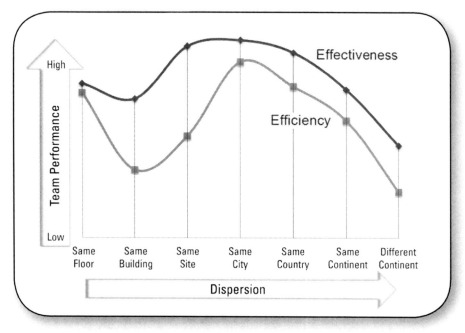

Figure 1-2: Performance generally degrades with time zone separation.
Adapted from Siebdrat, et al., 2009.[25]

Some Time Zone Remedies

THE MOTHER OF ALL TIME ZONE coordination remedies has always been hidden in plain view. It is not a technology or a complex process methodology. Instead, it is timeshifting. Global knowledge workers, from software engineers to marketing managers, adjust their "normal" working hours, creating one or more *overlap windows*. Timeshifting can be done occasionally (when needed, such as for a meeting) or systematically (e.g., every day).

From our years of studying this topic we have observed that nearly all dispersed groups practice at least some form of timeshifting at least some of the time. It is widespread because it is the key coordination solution for time-zone spanning teams as we found in every organization and project we studied. It is a new form of work design that global workers need to live with. Certainly, companies try to eliminate the need for timeshifting by routinizing tasks—structuring tasks as precisely as possible in order to eliminate the need for the knowledge workers to communicate across time zones. Then again, some work cannot be routinized and some tasks still need the occasional synchronizing conversation that resolves the burning question of "...

why didn't that work?" These conversations take place during the overlap, the *convergence window*, which we return to in chapter 3.

The most interesting of these timeshifters is the temporal liaison. The liaison is the critical person who bridges time zones and cultures, often by timeshifting every day. In fact, most global teams would not be able to function without such a liaison. This is why we see liaisons in nearly every global project team we have visited.

Some time zone remedies need to move beyond the team itself to the strategic level. Traditionally, decision makers paid scant attention to time zones when designing their distributed organization or when choosing sites or acquiring small firms. Now there seems to be more awareness regarding "time zone choice," the temporal analog to the geographical "location choice." Usually, time zone positioning implies clustering sites that are close in their time zones in order to overlap as much as possible. An organization could also design its entire environment and workflow around time zones and use one of the radical time zone strategies that we present later in the book: Follow-the-Sun, Round-the-Clock, or "Real-Time Simulated Co-location." Each of these strategies utilizes time in different ways for different objectives.

ACTIONABLE ITEMS

At the end of most of the chapters in this book we summarize the chapter with some practical, actionable suggestions that can be used in your organization today. All are based on the core information in that chapter.

- **Calendar differences.** At each location, conduct a detailed inventory of the six calendar differences (daily work hours, lunchtime, weekends, holidays, vacations, and equatorial). Share this inventory across the organization.
- **Scattertime.** Understand the scattertime in your organization. Survey the individual scattertimes. Get a sense of the best work times, possible work times, and "do not bother me" work times. Document these on the group work website.
- **Zoners.** Identify zoners in your organization and have them mentor others in time zone skills.

continued...

- **Meeting planning.** Use web-based tools to find optimal time windows for global meetings. Set up regular weekly global meeting schedules. Democratize the pain by rotating meeting times.
- **Timeshifting.** Map out the necessary timeshifting in order to optimize work time overlap and the coordination of work across sites.

CHAPTER 2

The Topography of Time Zone Dispersion

The Topography of Time Zone Dispersion

Jiri manages a far-flung group with two teams in Asia, two teams in the Americas, one in Israel, and one individual working solo in Florida (see fig. 2-1). Jiri struggles with time zones, specifically with issues of passing work between sites, setting up task collaboration, and scheduling meetings. Jiri hasn't analyzed the time zone differences or the work shift schedules. He admits that he had given so little thought to time zones that it was already a few weeks into the project before he calculated the group's time zone span.

JIRI IS A COMPOSITE of the overextended project manager for whom better time zone visualization can lead to his making better decisions. In order to illustrate dispersion for Jiri, our objective in this short chapter is to present the topography of time zone differences. We will do this by focusing on the key factors and configurations that influence time zone differences.

When people think about the time zone challenge, the first thing that probably comes to mind is the time difference between two locations. The practical solutions in such a case are relatively simple and often involve some timeshifting. However, with an increase in the number of locations and time zones, the complexity rises quickly and becomes daunting. As a result, timeshifting becomes harder to picture.

To illustrate the topography throughout this chapter, we use a *base case* we call Project Coraggio (in fig. 2-1), an amalgamation of a typical dispersed tech team. This is a project team located

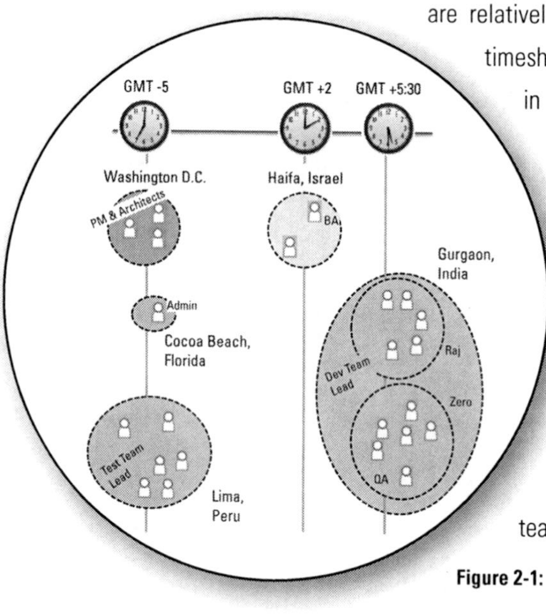

Figure 2-1: Bubble chart of time zone dispersion.[26]

22

in five clusters: a project manager (PM) and system architects are in Washington, D.C. at Firm Alpha; business analysts (BA) in Haifa, Israel at Firm Bravo; a development team in Gurgaon, India which is split between two buildings inside a high-tech park at Firm Bravo (the buildings on the Indian campus are named Raj and Zero); a test team in Lima, Peru at Firm Bravo; and a system administrator in Cocoa Beach, Florida, who is an independent contractor. We begin this chapter with four main factors that generate complexity in time zone dispersed environments.

What Drives Complexity in Time Zone Dispersion?

THE COMPLEXITY WE MENTIONED is a function of many factors, but research has identified four key factors that impact this complexity: team size, number of geographic locations, number of time zones, and time zone span. (Later in Appendix C, "Time Dispersion Indicators," these four factors are used to compute indicators of time zone dispersion.)

Team Size. In the Coraggio base case there are twenty-three team members. As Brooks[27] already concluded many years ago, adding more team members to a problematic project only makes matters worse because of the increased coordination overhead. The root of Brooks' seminal observation is that a team of size n can have as many as $n(n-1)/2$ possible communication and dependency links. Therefore, as the team grows in size, the coordination challenges grow exponentially. Herbsleb and colleagues[28] found, surprisingly, that geographic dispersion per se did not have a direct effect on software development speed; instead, dispersion required *larger* teams. This was mostly due to redundant roles, such as liaisons, at each site. Consequently, these larger teams led to lower productivity. With Gopal and colleagues[29] we found a U-shaped effect in relation to team size. Increasing team size improves dispersed software development speed up to a certain point, but after that, further increases in team size reduce development speed.

Number of Locations. In the Coraggio base case there are five locations. The number of locations is based on the assumption that team Raj and team Zero are in adjacent locations. However, if they were on different campuses, the locations for each team should then probably be viewed as separate, meaning the number of locations in this case would change to six. The number of locations is important because between each work site and each isolated individual there is an invisible communication and coordination barrier that needs to be bridged. All else being equal, the number of sites increases the degree of team dispersion and, consequently, the communication and coordination barriers in a global work environment.

Number of Time Zones. The Coraggio case has just three time zones since three of the five locations are all aligned in GMT -5. This number is not static, though; it changes several times each year when the United States and Israel, respectively, go in and out of DST (India and Peru have no DST).

This parameter represents the number of *distinct* time zones in which the team operates. While the number of locations increases the geographic dispersion of the group, such dispersion will have more dramatic effects when the respective locations are in different time zones. Generally speaking, as the number of time zones increases so does the complexity of the task context because members need to process more information cues (like "What time is it in location X?" or "When do our work hours overlap with location Y?") in carrying out the task.

Time Zone Span. The Coraggio base case operates between GMT -5 and GMT +5:30; thus, the time zone span is 10.5. The time zone span represents the maximum time zone difference spanned by any two individuals on the team, and therefore its maximum value is twelve. The time zone span affects the window of opportunity for same-time or synchronous interaction. While the Coraggio case operates in three distinct time zones, there is no work time overlap between the Americas and India; and there is no time for members of all three sites to meet synchronously without timeshifting.

Six Basic Time Zone Configurations

THE FACTORS ABOVE COMBINE to form what we call "time zone configurations." Over the years our research has identified six basic time zone configurations (fig. 2-2). We see these as basic, or "primitives," because these six configurations are not defined by other configurations. We also see these six as exhaustive and that other configurations are hybrids or special cases of these six "primitives." The advantage of understanding these configurations is that they tell a rich story, time zone-wise. If, for example, you managed a "far-flung" team (which is the last team in the list below) and then later you became involved in another team with that same configuration, then your range of managerial challenges and solutions would end up being similar.

The six configurations are presented here, arranged roughly in order of complexity.

Co-located. All team members work at the same location. The number of locations and time zones is one and the time zone span is zero. Note that a location could mean the same building, same campus or same city since there is no time separation.

North–South. Some team members are separated by distance but their work hours fully, or almost fully, overlap (e.g., Washington, D.C. with Lima, Peru). As we noted in chapter 1, DST complicates these computations. Furthermore, DST doesn't capture all the changes. While Peru doesn't have an official DST, many Peruvian organizations instead change their summer work hours to a summer schedule, *horario de verano*. When the summer schedule is in effect, workdays typically begin very early, include a very short lunch break, and then end early.

East–West. Team members are located in two or three cities with little or no time zone overlap. This is typical of Asian-American collaboration. East–West is a desirable configuration for Follow-the-Sun or Round-the-Clock strategies in which the task/product is handed off from one site to the next to achieve calendar efficiencies and improve development speed.

Clustered (also called "dispersed but concentrated" and "hub and spoke"). Members work in various locations and time zones, but there is one central, dominant site where a large percentage of members are located. The others, outside the cluster, are called "satellites." This configuration is typical of organizations working with various specialists in different locations. One of the special, interesting subsets of the clustered configuration is when the satellites are isolates—working solo. Such is the case with the Florida person in the Coraggio base case. Given that the isolates don't deal with anyone in their own location, all their communication is from afar.

Bridged (also called "lynch pin"). Two sites with no time zone overlap are connected via a liaison, a person who overlaps both sites. This liaison may be located in an in-between time zone. Alternatively, the liaison may be located at one of the two sites while doing substantial timeshifting. In social network parlance, this liaison has very high "betweenness centrality"— i.e., the effectiveness of the entire team is highly dependent on the effectiveness of the liaison to coordinate the work. As we noted in chapter 1, our research found that when there is no work time overlap, coordination delays occur, which is why appointing a liaison is recommended.

Far-flung. Individuals are widely scattered across various locations and time zones. This configuration is typical in organizations that are highly globalized and geographically dispersed, such as Intel and IBM, where work tends to be organized based on the talent needed for the task rather than on the location.

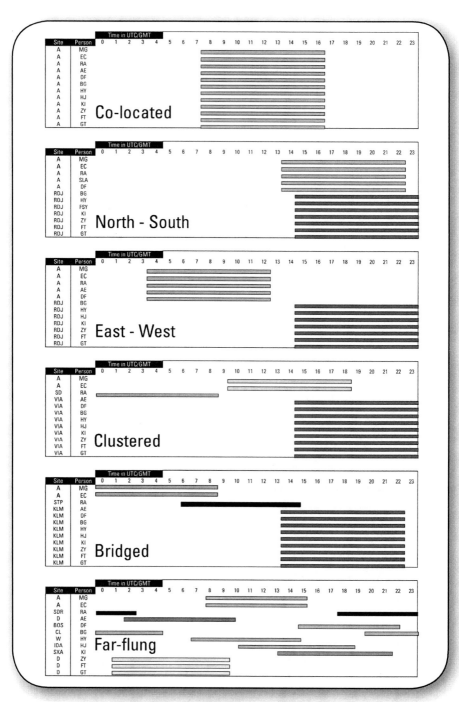

Figure: 2-2: Six basic time zone configurations.

Time Zone Diagrams

THE OLD ADAGE OF A PICTURE being worth a thousand words applies to the general understanding of time zone indicators and configurations. Decisions can be aided substantially with the use of graphics, visuals, parameters, and data. In our own research with Pickering,[30] we found that managers make better decisions when they are presented with visualization of time zone configurations. We now discuss charts and graphics used to represent time zone dispersion in global work environments.

Time zone line chart

The first step in thinking about the time zone configuration for an organizational team is to plot out a 24-hour line chart as shown in figure 2-3. Each site, with each individual who works at that site, is charted. In this depiction one can see each individual's hours. In order to be useful, this line chart needs to be enhanced by showing the timeshifting, which is the topic of our next chapter. The de facto timeshifting, including regular overtime hours, gives a better visual of the actual overlap.

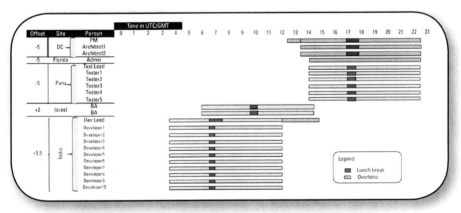

Figure 2-3: Basic line chart of time zones plus adjustment for overtime.
The work hours are shown using UTC/GMT, the absolute reference point of time.
Thus, the first person listed, the Project Manager (PM) in Washington D.C. begins work at 13:00 UTC/GMT (notice that she begins earlier than her teammates). The offset shown is -5, and therefore the PM begins at 13:00 – 5:00 = 08:00, or 8 a.m local time, in Washington D.C.

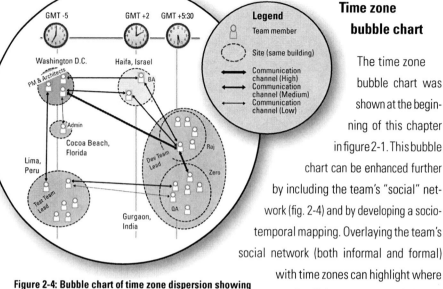

Time zone bubble chart

The time zone bubble chart was shown at the beginning of this chapter in figure 2-1. This bubble chart can be enhanced further by including the team's "social" network (fig. 2-4) and by developing a socio-temporal mapping. Overlaying the team's social network (both informal and formal) with time zones can highlight where overlap links are most needed.

Figure 2-4: Bubble chart of time zone dispersion showing a network diagram depicting main interdependencies. The chart can be enhanced by setting the arrow weights proportional to the level of communication (shown) or by color-coding (not shown).

ACTIONABLE ITEMS

- **Inventory of actual work hours.** Plot each and every team member's actual work hours on a line chart and then consider what can be done to increase overlap.
- **Think.** Think about your team configurations using the four factors, six configurations, bubble chart and line charts.
- **Document and compare.** Keep track of best and worst practices for every project and compare their similarities and differences within similar and dissimilar configurations.

CHAPTER 3

Timeshifting—
The Mother of
All Solutions for
Time Zone Differences

Timeshifting—
The Mother of All Solutions
for Time Zone Differences

Timeshift Anecdote #1: *Frank Li, a software engineer and trainer at IBM Chengdu in China, had to timeshift regularly. He was routinely scheduled for the **second shift**. Why? Because he was collaborating with the Americans who are eight to eleven hours away, and supposedly everyone involved in this collaboration was using agile software development methodology, which requires synchronized work.*

Timeshift Anecdote #2: *From an interview with a ChromatCity tech manager: "Most of the employees at ChromatCity here in Israel practice a **post-dinner shift** for quick e-mail review and updates in order to sync with California."*

TIMESHIFTING SIMPLY MEANS adjusting one's work hours to better sync with someone else's work hours. People timeshift in order to interact, and they interact in order to better coordinate their work across time zones. They talk by voice or Skype, quickly exchange text using e-mail or instant messaging (IM), or perhaps use a higher resolution telepresence meeting.

Timeshifting is but a modern instance of the more familiar *shiftwork*, something many professions have long required. Bakers of bread have been waking up in the early morning for many centuries to bake bread. In more recent centuries, hospital workers have worked shifts in order to be able to treat their patients twenty-four hours a day. Modern shiftwork originated with the modern factory, which required expensive resources of steel, production lines, and motors. In 1914, with a population demanding more automobiles, Henry Ford, founder of the Ford Motor Company, introduced three eight-hour shifts to achieve round-the-clock assembly in an automobile factory.[31] The themes and lessons from traditional shiftwork permeate this chapter.

Millions of knowledge workers are timeshifters now. In India, many software professionals regularly stay late at the office to overlap a bit with the U.S. workday. Even in Brazil, which overlaps significantly with most of its foreign partners, we found pervasive *ad-hoc* timeshifting and 19% of our sample had *routine* timeshifting.

Timeshifting is rampant because it is the key coordination solution for teams that span time zones, as we found in nearly every organization and project we have studied over the years. It is a new form of work design that global workers need to live with. It is rather mundane; it does not necessarily rely on the latest gadget, yet it is the essential first step to understanding time zone solutions.

While nearly all global workers do it, it is barely acknowledged from a managerial perspective.[32] Why is timeshifting under-acknowledged and understudied?[33] Perhaps it's due to the fact some view it as being in an embarrassing situation. Managers might not want to acknowledge how much timeshifting their employees do, in part because it appears exploitive. Separately, workaholics do not want to acknowledge how much they work during non-traditional times.

At the outset, we emphasize our first fundamental recommendation based on our time zone research. Do it! Even some timeshifting is beneficial. Why is timeshifting the mother of all solutions for global work across time zones? Because there is no other substitute for it, as expressed nicely by a seasoned tech executive who said to us, "...overlap is important. It's important to talk to people—you need to counsel them, to advise them, to control them, to supervise them. There's more openness when you talk to them. And you need to do knowledge transfer."

The magic of conversation is that it is better at getting individuals to synchronize their work. Collaborators need to *converge* on difficult problems such as the following: They need to agree on or build the same "mental model" in their minds; they need to resolve miscommunication issues; and, they need to coordinate activities between sites. They also need to conduct handovers between shifts and convey knowledge. All of these are more difficult over slow async e-mail. For all these reasons we call this overlap window the *convergence window*. It is quite useful to just have an open time period to allow any party to launch an easy, spontaneous conversation. If one side is stuck, or just wants to say hello and catch up, there would be a channel to chat in real time. Aside from the spontaneity, the handoff is another vital part of the convergence window because of the dialogue that happens. We elaborate on the handoff later in this chapter.

Let's look at Coolsand, at a typical global firm's timeshifting practices.

CASE STUDY
Coolsand Technologies

Coolsand[34] is a System on a Chip (SoC) company with 300 employees. Key R&D workers are in three time zones. Its two main centers are in Beijing (GMT +8) and France (GMT +1). The third site, at the time of the case, was the home of the American CTO (Chief Technology Officer) living in California (GMT -8) who addressed the overlap need by breaking up his workday.

Coolsand is typical of global firms in that its organizational design did not include any time zone planning. The three-site global configuration was determined largely by capital funding, personal connections, and ethnic roots. The configuration in figure 3-1 is the stepping-stone for the architecture of the work—how tasks are allocated between the sites.

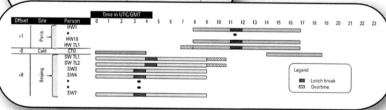

Figure 3-1: Coolsand's configuration in bubble diagram and line chart
(the latter is only a partial view of the project members).

The boundaries of task allocation were quite clear between the sites in China and France because they corresponded to the product architecture. The French

continued...

designed the hardware—the Integrated Circuit (IC) and certain software drivers. The Chinese designed most of the software, including the application layer on top of the IC. This architecture decoupled many interactions between sites and reduced much, though not all, need for synchronicity. However, it is natural to have design problems in the interface layers. When this happens, the sites do need to sync; the engineers need to have same-time dialogue.

In this case, it was possible to have a natural overlap between China and France of about two hours, if both locations timeshifted slightly—if the French arrived by 09:00 and the Chinese left a bit after 17:00. But this slight change was more difficult for the French to make than it might seem. The French engineers were somewhat reluctant to arrive earlier because it would get in the way of other morning routines such as taking the kids to school. Only two French engineers agreed to timeshift this way. About ten to fifteen Chinese engineers stayed late every day, often until 20:00 or even until 21:00, especially for the occasional videoconference.[35]

As with any shift design, eating norms became part of the story. When the Chinese engineers stayed late, the engineering manager sent the secretary to get dinner. On the other hand, the French engineers were often so busy during the morning overlap with their Chinese partners that they complained they didn't have time to get lunch.

Meanwhile, on the third continent, the California CTO broke up his daily work schedule into two smaller shifts: one in the early morning to overlap with the French engineers and the second in the afternoon to be available to the Chinese engineers. He used the middle of the day to exercise, take care of errands, or catch a quick siesta. His work schedule is a typical *scattertime* schedule and his role was somewhat similar to the bridged configuration depicted in figure 2-2 in chapter 2.

While there were overlaps built into this time zone configuration, inter-site problem solving was done mostly by e-mail. This was not so much due to time zones but rather because of language. While the company language is English, the Chinese engineers needed more time with English than the French engineers. This made spoken communication time consuming. On the other hand, e-mails

continued...

allowed individuals to read and respond at their own pace.

Language differences, coupled with built-in delay of time zone separation meant problem solving often took days or even a week. E-mail dialogue was often not specific enough, leading to another round of questions and clarifications. Time zone separation required the company to establish its "escalation processes," classifying an urgent problem and gathering the decision makers and experts to address the problem in a virtual meeting. Indeed, on occasion difficult problems were escalated to a videoconference. However, Coolsand was generally reluctant to do impromptu, off-hour meetings for quick synchronous problem solving, and there were no formal methods to get the engineering teams to quickly converge when problems arose. Instead, the interaction tended to stay in the slow back-and-forth e-mail channel of communication.

During particularly urgent project periods, Coolsand flew four or five of its key French engineers to China for several weeks at a time. However, once the global recession of 2008-09 arrived, the company reduced travel and tried to rely more on videoconferencing.

The Handoff

OUR SECOND FUNDAMENTAL RECOMMENDATION is to create a formal handoff routine as part of the convergence time window. The handoff transfers and resolves the essential information for all unfinished work. Without this handoff, project teams are more likely to suffer miscommunication and delays. We see formal handoffs in many global software engineering configurations that we visit. Jim Walsh, CTO of GlobalLogic, a global software firm, insists, "Make sure there is a one-hour handoff that is very formalized."

In fact, as we have discovered, the handoff is vital in many industries outside the technology world.[36] In order to better understand time zone-challenged work, we studied the shiftwork of other traditional knowledge workers such as hospital nurses. There we learned about the formality of the handoff between workshifts. For example, nurses in American hospitals typically have a thirty-minute overlap between shifts during which the outgoing nurse briefs the incoming nurse. The briefing is often done verbally, one-on-one, and combined with a written component that includes text and charts. In other words, these knowledge shift workers have a structured handover process that is routinely followed every day in every shift transfer. The transfer of knowledge, then, is in both verbal and written form. The written component is structured and uses templates but has a high degree of free flow natural language text.

Nevertheless, the handoff only addresses some of the coordination challenges. The language challenge was already illustrated in the Coolsand case earlier in this chapter. A related challenge is culture. For example, in a hierarchical culture such as the Indian culture where the boss and the subordinates are more distant, more instruction may be required during handoff relative to a more initiative-taking culture such as the American culture. Cultural and language differences mean that the handoff needs to be longer. Consequently, the convergence window may need to be expanded.

Shift Design and Night Shift

GLOBAL ORGANIZATIONS ARE INCREASINGLY dealing with another corollary of timeshifting, *shift design*, which means the scheduling of work shifts. While shift design for globally distributed workers is new, there are lessons in shift design from the "old days" of factory and service work evidenced by the terms in figure 3-2.

- **Shiftwork** is any nonstandard work schedule designed for work hours that stretch beyond the typical daylight periods of 07:00 to 18:00.
- **Rotating shift** is a work schedule designed for hours that change regularly as, for example, from day shift to evening shift to night shift. Rotation may be rapid (e.g., within three days), mid-length (e.g., one week) or long (e.g., four weeks) and rotate forward or backward.
- **Fixed shift** is a work schedule that remains the same from day to day.
- **Irregular shift** is a work schedule that is variable and erratic.
- **Night shift**, also known as *graveyard shift*, extends through the late night and early hours of the morning such as from 23:00 to 07:00.

Figure 3-2: The traditional language of shifts.[37]

Richard Coleman,[38] in his book about designing shifts and schedules, has one key message to the reader: Ultimately, it is about making sure that the workers are comfortable with the shift design solutions. In traditional shiftwork, most employees try to wrangle their way out of inconvenient shifts. The less convenient the shift, the more difficult it is to incentivize and manage the shift.

The shirking of night shift work is now occurring in India and elsewhere where there is a newly empowered and confident workforce. When the American software firm CLX tried to institute 24/7 support from India, CLX managers carefully planned a work schedule of five shifts, taking into consideration all overlap and vacation times. But this carefully laid out plan unraveled because the employees on the night shifts would quit. At the global firm Axtended Software, there was an early period of experimentation with night shift work at its large Indian location. However, this effort was disappointing because of higher turnover and performance problems so the company decided to minimize night work at its India location whenever possible. A Pakistani tech company, TenPearls, ran a night shift for several years and discovered that workers became unhealthy and that employee turnover increased. In all three cases, the night shift was eliminated. These timeshifting organizations all reacted similarly. After the night shift failure, they each set up creatively designed day shifts that stretched from early mornings for the first shift through late evening for the last shift, with some overlap periods.

When many employees are involved, shift schedule design software comes to the rescue. For example, at Sutherland Global Services, a BPO (Business Process Outsourcing) firm, the shift schedule design of its huge Philippine and Indian centers is intricate. The shifts, which are determined by business demand, are staggered every fifteen minutes. The shift schedule is designed by a workforce management system based primarily on transportation optimization with these key parameters: location of worker, what time the worker is picked up, the time the worker will arrive at the office, the nine-hour shift span and the drop-off time.

The Basic Parameters of Timeshifting

THE FOUR PARAMETERS IN PLANNING and designing timeshifting arrange nicely to the mnemonic **SHIFt:**

- **S – Standardized?** This refers to the rhythm of timeshifting. It asks whether timeshifting is ad hoc or regular. It is easier for both sides if an overlap window is routinely included. This will help create a particular rhythm of communication and workflow.

- **H – How long?** This is the duration of the convergence window. Is a thirty-minute overlap sufficient for a quick handoff or should it be a three-hour window of open availability? Yahoo Boston instituted "Norway Days," when its American software engineers, collaborating with a Norwegian team, allocated a few days each week to begin at 05:30; nearly an entire workday of overlap was created as a result.

- **I – Number of individual participants.** This asks who will be timeshifting: Is it one key person at a site, some, or all? We call the key person the *temporal liaison* and we introduce him/her later in this chapter.

- **F – Frequency.** This asks how many times per day/week timeshifting should occur. It could be twice a week such as the Pakistani–American collaboration at TenPearls where the routine was every Tuesday and Friday at 08:00 Washington, D.C. time and 18:00 Karachi time. It could happen daily, coupled with a fifteen-minute meeting, like a Russian–Swiss collaboration that we came across. Niksun, a U.S.-based software company that conducts quick cycles on its software R&D, launched an even more ambitious timeshifting scheme consisting of two overlapping meetings per day between the United States and India: one early in the morning and one at night.

Beyond SHIFt, there are many variations within a firm. Some teams timeshift more than others; seasons require adjustments because of DST; or, there are differences by task and by phase. There is operational timeshifting versus R&D. In some companies, various support and infrastructure units regularly assign one or two employees to work in nontraditional shifts.

How to Create and Lengthen the Overlap Convergence Window

IN MANY CASES THE DISTANT SITES want to extend the overlap window, perhaps from one hour to three hours. There are actually quite a few options for increasing the convergence time window between time-separated partners.

One option involves flextime or telework. Flextime (flexible working schedules) and telework (working from home) are more common in wealthier nations. Governments have been advocating telework for decades now in the United States, Britain, and in several other nations. Approximately 40% of the workforce has jobs that could be performed remotely, at least part of the time.[39] American firms are realizing that flextime gives the firm greater time zone reach. For example, BPO work such as call center work is increasingly being done from home. Individuals commute to a quiet room in their house and work from there. One American company, oDesk, is rather strict. The company uses sophisticated monitoring software to keep track of every time segment that the employee is on the clock. With this device, oDesk is able to discourage employees from leaving their desks while working at home, and distractions like Facebook are kept at bay.

A second option involves scattertime. Scattertime, the splintering of work time, is a direct result of flextime. Given that scattertime is common in global firms, it makes the burden of timeshifting both easier and harder. It is easier because individuals have the technology and the flexibility. It is harder because it is more difficult to find just the right window for synchronous meetings when individuals on a project team are scattered geographically and are working nontraditional hours.

In emerging or developing countries, these norms of working from home, scattertime, and nomadism are all less popular. There are several reasons for this. Homes are more crowded and noisy; local managers want to keep an eye on their employees since they are much more likely to have second jobs and there is a possibility that they will devote more energy to their moonlighting job for which they receive higher pay. Separately, foreign clients may contractually restrict offsite work for security reasons related to intellectual property theft, or financial crime concerns.

A different option is to extend the workday span through creative tinkering. An "8-hour workday" spans more than 8 hours due to lunch breaks. By instituting a 1-hour lunch, the site can grab a little bit more overlap time at one of the edges. Similarly, a four-day workweek with more hours in each workday may be just the right thing for some collaborative projects. It is important to remember that not all workweeks are 40 hours. For example, some Brazilian companies work the official 8.8 hours per day.

Then there is overtime, which, while less appealing, is an effective way to increase the time window. Some companies pay overtime, others just expect it. In some nations, labor regulations restrict overtime, while in others it is the norm. In some cases, weekend work may be useful. And then there are personal preferences regarding overtime. We usually hear that there is more willingness to stay late rather than to arrive very early. For example, in a Portuguese–Brazilian collaboration we studied, the Portuguese individuals didn't mind staying late. They thought it easier to extend their day instead of making the Brazilians wake up earlier for the meeting.

Paradoxically, scheduling at the "edges" of the day may be difficult. The edge may be 09:00 or 17:00. At first either seems like a perfectly reasonable time slot for time zone overlap. However, as John Tang and colleagues[40] at Microsoft Research found, these are actually inconvenient times for many knowledge workers because they conflict with non-work issues such as child pick-up/drop-off or commuting schedules. Instead, these knowledge workers prefer to meet from home either earlier or later. This blurs traditional workdays and makes them look more like scattertime.

Managers need to work on minimizing the timeshifting pain of meetings. If employees are timeshifting from the office, managers can make the office much more palatable by throwing in inexpensive perks. These might include buying breakfast for employees who come in early or ordering taxis for those who stay late. We will return to this subject in chapters 7 and 8.

Finally, if timeshifting is the mother of all solutions, how much of it is needed? How much of a convergence window is necessary? Regrettably, there is no formula that says that four hours is twice as valuable as merely two hours. The time window size depends on the work, the tasks, the processes, the people, and more. Later, in chapter 7, we offer a radical strategy of complete overlap called Realtime Simulated Co-location. But this radical strategy certainly isn't necessary for most global collaboration.

Meet the Key Timeshifter:
the Temporal Liaison

THE MOST INTERESTING AND PREVALENT timeshifter is the *temporal liaison*, the person who bridges time zones. Global knowledge collaborations such as software projects would not function without such liaisons. After all, they serve as cultural and organizational bridges, a vital role in addition to their temporal function. We found liaisons in nearly every global project team we studied, and we recommend that no globally dispersed project should be without at least one temporal liaison.[41] You will recognize the temporal liaison when you meet the person who stretches, shifts, and scatters his hours to create work time overlap with both his co-located colleagues and his distant colleagues.

The liaison is so universal that the job has many names such as: point of contact, bridge, window man, the "OC" (On-site Coordinator, a term used at the Indian IT company Infosys), go-between, and boundary spanner. At Microsoft, in software work that uses distributed agile development, the liaison may be called the team-room buddy.[42] Regardless of the title, the liaison relies heavily on real-time channels, namely voice calls to the office or to a mobile device. The liaison knows when to step in and do something different to advance communication and move the task forward.

The liaison is typically a mid-level manager such as a project manager. We see this management role as representing a change in how effective managers operate. A few decades ago the dictum was MBWA, Management By Wandering Around, wherein managers relied on face-to-face contact and discussions with subordinates. Then in the 1990s it became MBFA, Management By Flying Around; and now it's MBTA, Management By Timeshifting Around.[43]

The liaison is a frontline job, nicely illustrated by a narrative from an Israeli CTO living in Silicon Valley who served as a liaison between the American site and the Israeli R&D center ten hours away.[44] He said, "to be an Israeli in Silicon Valley and to collaborate with Israel means that you have to live every day twice: once during the day and once again at night." In one incident, the CTO, so as not to wake his wife and children, took a stroll outside his suburban house very late at night in order to conduct a three-way voice meeting with Japan and Israel. A police car soon appeared, siren blaring. The policeman explained that the neighbors were particularly anxious because the CTO was speaking in a strange language on a night soon after the 9/11 terrorist attacks in the United States.

These kinds of frontline liaisons self-select into globalized work that requires timeshifting, and they often thrive in these positions. Such shiftwork choices were partially confirmed in a study conducted by Baker and colleagues.[45] These researchers found that there was a dramatic difference in workers' personal preferences about schedule choices between day workers and shift workers, though the reasons for the difference were not clear. This is how researchers summarized the workers' tastes:

> **"** It is possible that individuals who are already more flexible regarding work hours are drawn to, or more successful at shiftwork. Alternatively, individuals may learn to value time differently after being involved in irregular working time arrangements. The question remains, however, whether shift workers have a wider range of preferences

for work time because they are shift-workers, or whether they are shift-workers because they are prepared to work at a wider range of times."

Nevertheless, even with self-selection, we have noticed that liaisons gripe about the time inconvenience. For example, one Brazilian liaison we interviewed for our study expressed annoyance that he had to be on call all the time and had to take lunch by himself at a different time from the rest of his staff.

More on Handoffs in Traditional Shiftwork

THE HANDOFF IS CLEARLY one of the most important dimensions of shiftwork in knowledge industries, distributed or otherwise. The stories and lessons from the world of traditional shiftwork give all of us some perspective on how to think about the timeshifting solutions and risks.

We begin with catastrophes. All the famous catastrophic industrial accidents of the late 1900s happened during night shifts or stemmed from poor handoff between shifts. Most prominent of these was the Exxon Valdez oil tanker spill of 1989 in Alaska where the accident happened during a shift change.[46] Another oil related accident was the Piper Alpha North Sea disaster of 1988. There is an enormous amount of information to relay from shift to shift on large offshore oil platforms. Unfortunately, the transfer of knowledge from one shift crew to another crew failed in both cases. In part, the situation was exacerbated by poor communication between subcontracted workers as this excerpt relates:

At about 6pm on July 6, 1988 [day shift] workers on the oil platform Piper Alpha sought permission to stop work on the backup propane condensate pump, leaving a hole in the pump where a valve had been. Just before 10pm the primary propane condensate pump failed. Workers on the next shift were unaware that the backup pump was inoperative, and started the backup pump.

The first explosion was caused by gas escaping from the hole in the pump where the valve should have been, and was followed 20 minutes later by a larger explosion. [...] The fire was visible from 85 miles and felt at one mile away. Almost all of the platform was melted off down to sea level. 167 personnel died, 165 out of the 226 on board the platform, plus two from a rescue vessel.47 (emphasis added by authors)

Not all handoffs are catastrophic of course. It is the routine of handoffs that is of interest in this chapter. Hospital nurses pass on data about a patient under treatment, 24-hour news desks pass information along about the latest piquant story, and police detectives pass on information about a hot case. More on the first two types of handoffs follows.

Hospital nurses in the United States used to have traditional work schedules of three shifts of eight hours. Nowadays the schedules are different. The shift-work schedule was redesigned because hospitals came to the conclusion that three shifts per day is a bad idea for patients and hinders "continuity of care." Accordingly, now the work schedule usually consists of two long shifts of twelve hours each: 07:00 to 19:00 and 19:00 to 7:00.

In practice, each shift is formally 12.5 hours because the last 30 minutes are used as overlap time with the next shift. That is when handoff takes place—when the outgoing nurse gives the briefing to the incoming nurse. The briefing is done verbally, one-on-one, augmented by a written component that includes text and charts. In some hospitals, the briefing is done as a group. Each nurse gives a briefing on his/her patients to all the unit's nurses because it is better for patients that all the nurses have a good mental picture of everything that is happening on the floor. But this, of course, takes much longer to do. In a very different take, some hospitals conduct the briefings via audio recording.

A typical handoff briefing involves a nurse with eight patients. At thirty minutes, that computes to two to four minutes per patient. Usually this does not allow enough time for the complete briefing. In some instances though, an hour for briefing may not be unusual with regard to patients with certain medical conditions. The "charting," the written report, is sometimes completed only during overtime because the nurse was too busy during her/his shift to document the story of each patient.

The handoff in the newsroom is no less profound. Similar to the foregoing hospital nurse case and cases involving other knowledge workers, each shift needs to handoff all of their works-in-progress—their hot stories, their tips, and their opinions. The U.S. news desk that we visited used three shifts of eight hours each, plus some overlap time for handoff. The knowledge was handed off between shifts using two key processes: a written document plus the verbal overlap dialogue between the two shift producers.

The written document is supposed to encompass everything: what news pieces are being prepared, what changes need to be made, what is in the news, things to know, and the highlights of each segment such as: "Secretary Clinton will talk with us live from her hotel." But the written document is not enough. After the incoming producer reads the document, she discusses it with the outgoing producer, and together they do the verbal part of the handoff. The incoming editor gets specific details and is able to ask questions. The verbal part "allows you to push back and ask questions" and to get the feel of the story's importance: "How hot is the story?" It is this last point that seems the most difficult to pass on from one shift to the next. A developing story is somewhat subjective and occasionally leads to misunderstandings between the shifts.

In summary, the common elements of the shift handoff for both nurses and journalists are twofold: written plus verbal. The written transfer is structured and uses templates but has a high degree of free flow natural language text. The verbal transfer ranges from thirty to sixty minutes, partially influenced by the personalities.

ACTIONABLE ITEMS

- **Open the window.** Strive for convergence windows, the overlaps across sites, by designing new shifts or encouraging flextime/scattertime.
- **Open the window wider.** Set up longer open overlap periods for unscheduled collaborative work, interactions, and questions.
- **Use the window.** Once you have worked so hard to timeshift, make sure that you benefit. For example, make sure all collaborators have IM or chat on, or even texting/SMS.
- **Formalize the handoff.** Formalize the handoff as part of the overlap period. Use a structured handoff process that is routinely followed every day at every shift transfer, including both a verbal and a written (template-based) transfer of knowledge.
- **Close the window.** Consider the converse—the need for some quiet time with no overlap so knowledge workers can focus better, uninterrupted.
- **Change the reward structure.** Communicate the availability of flextime and scattertime to your employees. Minimize the "counting hours" controls. Make it clear that employees are rewarded based on performance, not for sitting in the office.

continued..

- **Temporal liaisons.** Create temporal (time) liaisons at each site. These are the individuals who timeshift more than others.
- **Food.** Buy breakfast or dinner for employees who timeshift from the office.
- **Full employee input.** In designing shift schedules, make sure that the workers are comfortable with the shift schedule solutions.

CHAPTER 4

Solutions for Time Zones—
Sync or Async

Solutions for Time Zones— Sync or Async

There is no Moore's Law for time zones.

THERE ARE NO MIRACLE TECHNOLOGIES to overcome time zone differences. While knowledge workers are spoiled with exponential technology improvements à la Moore's Law, such changes are not in the offing to address time zone differences. Even the use of fancy videoconferencing or 3G holography cannot overcome the fundamental time zone difference problem which led to the title of this book "I'm Working While They're Sleeping...." The challenges of time zone separation can be mitigated but cannot be eradicated.

What makes up the palette of coordination tools and tactics to mitigate the problems of time zones? This chapter reveals the full palette in one place. These coordination tactics were compiled from both our own research and research done by others.

Global collaborators interact using a combination of two modes: sync or async. In this chapter we answer two key questions. The first is: "Are you doing the maximum during synchronous (sync) overlap time?" Sync interaction tends to be less structured. It is best used for converging on fuzzy and difficult issues. Recall that this is why the overlap period is called the convergence window.

Second, we answer the converse: "Are you doing the maximum during non-overlap time, asynchronous (async) time, in structuring the work in order to facilitate the workflow, transmit knowledge, and plan the handoffs between distant sites?"

A balance is needed between sync and async. Some argue that sync is more desirable, but this is not always the case. Too much sync time may lead to interruptions and over-coordination. Keep in mind that when team members are coordinating, their attention is diverted from the focal task. Async communication is most effective when transmitting information. Sync communication is most effective when the team is seeking convergence, as when having a discussion to resolve issues, reaching an agreement, or clarifying a prior miscommunication.

Sync, async, process, culture, technologies, and even individual quirks are all elements that need to be addressed in order for effective coordination to happen. Working in distributed collaboration requires extra energy as is described in the Intel case coming up later in this chapter. At that Intel engagement, the global team facilitator queried everybody: "What's your coordination style?" Unrushed, the team devoted plenty of time exploring how each person wanted to communicate, what was his/her preferred channel of communication, and how flexible the individual could be at various times of the day.

Working More Effectively
During Sync/Overlap Periods

THE OVERLAP IS THE TIME TO TALK or to text. Once the overlap periods are established in your organization, it is time to look at the technology. There are two applicable technologies for optimizing sync work: technology for communications and technology for awareness. The first, technology for communications, is the more intuitive one and we begin with it.

Over the years we have found that too many dispersed collaborations do not make sufficient use of common communication technologies and regress to the lowest common denominators of voice and e-mail. Project members should make systematic use of always-on messaging (IM/chat/text/SMS) for day-to-day communication and convergence. Of course, video is also used in some companies for remote meetings. Video use ranges from desktop solutions such as Skype, to the deluxe high-end HD videoconferencing (e.g., Telepresence from Cisco or Halo from HP). We expect some of the readers of this book in the year 2020 to be using 3D hologram projections of their colleagues whenever they have regularly scheduled meetings with them.

Second, and more subtle, are technological solutions for *awareness*. These tools are vital because when collaborators are actually overlapping in work hours, they should use that time to progress on the work that requires that special touch of person-to-person convergence. In order to do that, the initiating individual needs to be aware of the distant collaborator, just as if she could walk over to his desk. Therefore, in order to simulate these cues, key awareness indicators are needed that would tell a story of whether the distant collaborator is available at his desk, what he's working on, and whether it is okay to interrupt him. In addition to availability awareness, the tools can provide awareness of current work tasks, colleagues, and social networks—and even the weather. The most pervasive awareness indicators are the online status icons that are now integrated into many e-mail, IM, mobile chat, and VoIP suites with self-reporting indicators such as, "I am free for chat," "I am out at lunch" or even mood indicators like, "I am in a bad mood."

For the zoner in particular, awareness-related tools can include individual and global calendars, holiday schedules, or even desktop video cameras. One radical kind of awareness technology is to use always-on video, which we describe later in this chapter when we introduce the concept of Real-Time Simulated Co-location.

Awareness tools are becoming more pervasive and are part of the multi-functional "collaboration platforms" that larger global companies sew, glue, and package for their global staff. These days these collaboration platforms may also be rebranded as "mobility tools." For example, at U.S.-based Applied Materials the collaboration platform is called "Applied Anywhere." At IBM thousands of distributed workers have access to IBM's approved awareness technologies packaged for any individual or team that needs them.

Working More Effectively During Async/Non-Overlap Periods

FUNDAMENTALLY, ASYNC WORKFLOW is a more structured, mechanized, codified, and disciplined set of work processes. It has to be that way because collaborators cannot rely on the small adjustments that a human conversation can solve (because "they're sleeping"). At the extreme, there is no need at all for same-time voice communication, or text-based chat, since all the work can be done by structuring and allocating the work very carefully. The goal is to engineer everything so carefully that all possible miscommunications are eliminated and there is no need for sync voice clarifications. There's no need to talk to anyone far away. Ever. That's a tall order.

Eliminate the verbal all together?

Nevertheless, some exemplary sectors have come close to attaining the goal of eliminating verbal coordination. The first is in back-office work, also known as BPO, where billions of dollars' worth of work is now successfully handed off to Asian processing centers many time zones away (see chapter 6). All this happens quite successfully in fields such as insurance processing, accounting, and legal. The second sector is in the open source software community. Members of this community, who are far-flung and talk to each other infrequently, have been collaborating asynchronously and successfully for more than a decade, spinning out thousands of software products such as Firefox, Apache and Linux.

The extreme of no-communication across time zones is an interesting purist goal. We had the following interchange with the CTO of CLX, an American software company:

> *"The secret of overcoming time zone separation is to eliminate real-time communication as much as possible," said the CTO.*
>
> *"You mean minimize, correct?" probed the authors.*
>
> *"Yes, but really we try to eliminate," replied the CTO.*
>
> *He continued, "We have a scheduled hand-off point every day at, for example, 07:00 India time and there are no other communication points."*

As the dialogue illustrates, the goal is to be totally async with no overlap for verbal convergence.

Technology and process

What coordination activities can be done during the async period? A lot, actually. Any coordination involving the simple transmission of information can be done independently, without interaction. The conceptual term is *conveyance*. It is the notion of conveying information from one distant collaborator to another (more on this in chapter 10). Of course e-mail is an excellent tool for this.

A key element of any async process is the *escalation process*. These are the guidelines for taking action in crises, solving pressing problems and answering urgent questions. Clear escalation processes minimize the likelihood of a message bouncing around the world in search of the right person. Every global worker has a horror story of an important escalation that didn't work because it wasn't clear how to escalate, or the right person wasn't available, or the message sat in an inbox.

And now we come to the palette of technological solutions for async collaboration. Companies use project management and version control tools, global repositories ranging from Google Docs to SharePoint, continuous integration and bug reporting tools, and wikis. IBM has many nifty tools that it uses internally to support its highly distributed workforce. For example, *Collaboration Advisor* asks the users, as a group, a number of basic questions and then recommends tools to support their group work. India-based Infosys has fused its software methodologies into its async technology suites.

The choice of async workflow methodology that we mention is from the world of software work, but the principles apply to any knowledge collaboration. In the world of software, "architects" break up the software components as much as possible to make them as independent as possible such that distant sites do not have to communicate quite as much with each other. Resources and tasks are very carefully allocated by phase and by geography to minimize task dependencies, handoffs, and clarification requests.[48] We return to these principles in subsequent chapters.

Many software companies today tend to innovate around "agile" methodologies. Later in this book we introduce the "radical" strategies of Follow-the-Sun and Real-Time Simulated Co-location, two schemes that may be best implemented with agile software approaches. Agile may be more suited for coordinated work across distant time zones because the project team implements the "daily continuous integration," where all tasks get done and packaged before the end of a shift.[49]

Let's look at a large global firm and its handling of time zone challenges.

CASE STUDY
Intel

Intel is, and has been, one of the most highly distributed global corporations for about two decades. It has plants and R&D operations in many locations including the United States, Ireland, China, Israel, and Costa Rica.[50] Many of Intel's work teams have members far-flung across many time zones. While Intel still struggles with time zone differences, it does two things quite well. At the organizational level, it has many approaches and technologies to address time zone problems; at the individual level, many of its employees are already time zone seasoned and are what we call "zoners." Intel recognizes that time zones are a challenge and has had specialists working on process and technology solutions—which is one of the reasons we were invited to study the time zone challenges faced by their technical project teams.

continued...

Our case focuses on one team of fifteen individuals working on a budgeting application. The Intel Budget Resource (IBR) team was especially far flung. The team represented individuals in seven distinct time zones (eleven locations). The time zones ranged from GMT -8 (California) to GMT +8 (Shanghai) with a time zone span of 11.5. Given that it was such a far-flung team, there were no miracle time zone solutions. Here is how this Intel team mitigated the time zone challenges during this eight-month project that included Intel people and outside providers in Russia.

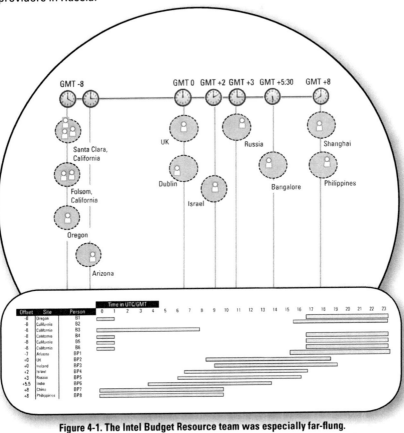

Figure 4-1. The Intel Budget Resource team was especially far-flung.
The team represented individuals in seven distinct time zones (11 locations).
Most of the Intel team worked during fairly conventional hours.
One pair in California timeshifted dramatically.

continued...

Let's begin with the most popular time zone solution, timeshifting. The special adaptation that this Intel team used for timeshifting was referred to as a "circular meeting" schedule. Individuals at each site timeshifted, at least somewhat. The goal was to increase work time overlap among those team members who needed to interact more frequently. The meeting schedule contained all meetings that would take place in a twenty-four-hour period. Meetings were scheduled on a continuous basis with different members meeting for specific purposes at pre-defined times around the clock.

Simply knowing a time of the day when a given team member could communicate with another with certainty seemed to be of great help for planning purposes. As one interviewee described: "Actually there's about four technical people that we meet with every morning at 05:00 [Pacific time] to review what progress [and] issues that we have seen from the previous day. Then we meet with our end users at 08:30 [Pacific time] and tell them what to test that day and any feedback from the technical team. And then we meet with the end users again at 15:30 [Pacific time] to get the test results and any feedback that they want us to give to the technical team the next morning." All meeting times were entered into a master schedule in the project repository so that everyone knew who would be meeting with whom and when.

One successful feature of this meeting scheme was the strict adherence to meeting times. One team member arriving five minutes late to a meeting could throw the meeting coordination into disarray. "Meetings get stopped because one of the key members isn't available at that specific time," said one of the technical personnel. Scheduling was challenging because there were some team members who were not assigned full-time to the project, and sometimes this meant that meeting timeslots were scheduled months in advance.

Despite the effectiveness of the circular meeting schedule, there were still some delays when a task or an individual member got out of sync with the team. As one interviewee commented, "some people are still working and others have already finished," which leads to additional effort and after business hours

continued...

work. In many cases team members needed to wait until the next day for a response due to time zone differences. Additionally, the circular meeting schedule could not address a need for the occasional all-members meeting across time zones when everyone needed to be present. The U.S. members were the ones who had to meet in the middle of the night.

The problem with timeshifting for this far-flung team was that each hour that was shifted by one individual increased overlap with some team members but decreased overlap with others. Another problem was that some team members found themselves working at off hours, which led to some burnout. One pair timeshifted radically—at a California site, two members rarely saw each other because one of them arrived at 04:00, while the other one worked late hours.

Of course, this meeting schedule was not the only technique that this Intel team used. The team also employed some technical solutions[51] and other practices and task organizational methods. For example, the overall meeting coordination design was hatched at the kick-off conference. The initial face-to-face meeting at the beginning of the project was intended to allow the group to coordinate the schedules for the project meetings in a way that was fair to everyone. Not only did this kick-off help coordination, but team members also got to know each other and learned about individual meeting preferences and work habits.

The kick-off meeting was also where the basic team repository was devised in order to keep everyone informed about all key aspects of the project. No action was taken and no decision was made without reviewing the repository and without logging an entry describing the action or decision into the repository. Similarly, all key meeting discussions, decisions and agreements were documented in the repository. There was also a tendency to over-detail the descriptions recorded to minimize the need for clarifications later on. The repository was an important part of the coordination process established by the team. For example, business analysts did not discuss issues directly with developers. Instead, they logged their issues in a central issue log in the repository so that developers could then meet and coordinate on how to address these issues most effectively. One team member

continued...

53

also maintained a dashboard in the repository for everyone to obtain updated task awareness information about key progress indicators for the project.

The team established a temporal liaison, a central coordinator, whose responsibility was to keep the project well synchronized. In addition, each location had an "assigned" project manager who served as a local coordinator so that team members in that location would know whom to talk to about project issues. Overall, most team members we interviewed were very satisfied with how the team coordinated its work. They also recognized the challenges of working across several time zones.

Social Media and Web 2.0

SOCIAL MEDIA TOOLS CREATE HIGHER LEVELS of mental synchronicity between individuals. Ergo, they are potentially useful to time zone challenges. Facebook has many of the capabilities that were already mentioned in this chapter: communication, presence awareness, social awareness, and information sharing. The tools are especially useful for instilling implicit, unspoken coordination. They allow users to figure out when they will be in the same city (Tripit) or when they are walking on the same block (Foursquare). The slightly older Web 2.0 tools based on microblogging or wikis can also address coordination across time zones. Microblogging services such as Twitter or Yammer, an enterprise version of Twitter, might be worthwhile for distant collaborators to use to increase awareness about each other, or they may prefer keeping up to date using automatic activity feeds like RSS. A sharing culture, so useful for time zone challenges, can emerge when workers have an easy way to share and when they trust that the sharing will be secure, appreciated, and reciprocated. As an added benefit, the deluge of e-mail may begin to diminish.

In sum, there is potential for social media having an impact on coordination across time zones, but so far we have seen little impact in the workplace. For example, by 2010 IBM had introduced its own internal "blue" versions of major social networking tools such as Twitter and Facebook. However, at "Big Blue" we did not find that such tools were being used as communication channels for multi-time zone collaboration. This is similar to what John Tang and his colleagues found in their study at Microsoft and other firms.[52]

The Four Levels of Time Zone Robustness

TIME ZONE ROBUSTNESS (TZR) is our maturity framework for examining time zone related processes. With our colleague Rafael Prikladnicki, we studied different software companies and found that they vary quite a bit in how well they integrate time zone challenges into their work design (the description here is an extension of our thinking from the Brazilian study[53]). We found, for instance, that while some firms maximize the use of the natural convergence time window, others are less aggressive. This led us to construct a model with four levels that describe and prescribe deliberate actions around time zone-driven collaboration.

In this model, Level 1 is the least developed, Level 4 the most developed. Level 1 organizations tend to be small and medium-sized companies that may have globalized recently. Level 2 organizations have the tools but are not using them fully, while Level 3 organizations represent the majority of larger global technology companies. We do not anticipate that entire organizations will function at Level 4, but teams, projects, or divisions that have been designed around time zones can function well at this highest level.

The four levels of robustness are described as follows:

- Level 1 – Ad-hoc. At this level, all time zone tactics are ad-hoc and reactive. Level 1 organizations rely mostly on async tools such as e-mail. This is the case not only because of cost considerations but also because of their traditional organizational mindset. Of course, voice communication, the key sync channel, is used, but not systematically.

- Level 2 – Tooled. Level 2 organizations regularly use synchronous tools (IM, chat, texting, screen sharing, video, awareness technologies) but their use is not systematic. There is some sporadic collaboration that takes place around rigorous workflow and leverages either the overlap or non-overlap portions of the workday, but this type of collaboration has not yet been routinized.

- Level – Holistic. Level 3 organizations recognize and implement a holistic approach to collaboration technologies and processes. They have state-of-the-art collaborative technology to support distributed teams and far-flung individuals. Awareness tools and status indicators are heavily used, especially various messaging tools such as chat. These have all become part of the organizational culture. Workflow processes are systematic for both sync and async portions of the workday.

- Level 4 – Leveraged. The Level 4 organizations design their environment and workflow around time zones. They take the fork in the road toward one of the following: distant, minimal communication strategies like Follow-the-Sun and Round-the-Clock (see chapter 6) in which, at the end of the day, work is passed to another global site many time zones away; or, complete time overlap which we label as "Real-Time Simulated Co-location" (see chapter 7) wherein the distant sites collaborate naturally as if co-located, partially based on always-on audio/video.

ACTIONABLE ITEMS

Work Methodology

- **Workflow**. Go to work on designing/structuring workflow as a key coordination tactic.
- **Dashboard**. Maintain a central log in which all activities and key task actions are captured and displayed. These logs can be wikis, tweets, blogs, and version control systems.
- **Handoff**. Formalize the handoff during the overlap period. It should include both a verbal and a written transfer of knowledge.
- **Async voice.** If there is no overlap, then key individuals in the outgoing shift can record handoff information via voicemail/videomail.
- **Escalation**. Design and practice bulletproof escalation processes. These are the guidelines for taking action in crises, solving pressing problems and answering urgent questions.

Technologies

- **Beyond e-mail.** Aggressively move to technologies beyond e-mail—wiki, document repositories, collaborative project management, group calendaring with strong time zone support—to address each kind of collaboration need. Establish a free organization-wide voice conferencing platform.
- **Methodology + Tech.** Move to systems that embed your organization's structured workflows.
- **Evaluate and move up**. Assess the TZR level at which your team or organization operates and make deliberate decisions to move up.

continued...

Awareness Approaches

- **Individual awareness.** Create easy access to personal and context information for collaborators. This could include current time, calendar, holiday schedule, and even the weather. There should also be a rich personal profile with a personal narrative. Other pertinent information that should be contained in the profile include best times to contact, working hours and additional ways a person can be reached. Make sure profiles are updated regularly.
- **Feeds and tweets.** Subscribe to activity feeds from colleagues. Create alerts of changes made to workspaces, pages, and blogs.

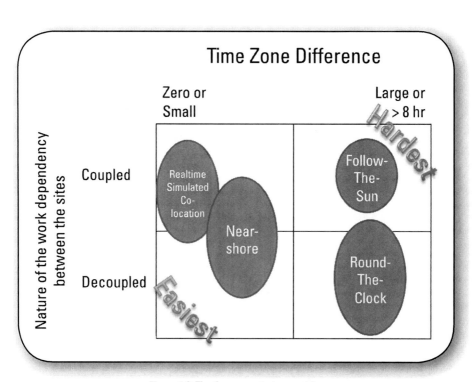

Figure 5-0: The time zone strategy matrix.

SECTION II
Time Zone Strategy

Time zone and strategy have not been fused together before in management books. Hence, in this section, we are sailing into new waters to look at time zones.

First, let's begin with the bedrock. Time zone strategy and the nature of the work are deeply intertwined, like the chicken and the egg question. They need to be examined together at the start. The time zone strategy matrix (fig 5.0) captures the intersection of time zones and the nature of the work, although not every concept we cover can be plotted into this two-dimensional matrix.

Chapter 5 is about location choice. We argue that "Time zones matter." just as much as the old adage "Location matters."

Chapter 6 presents approaches to leverage time zone separation, but for very different purposes. Follow-the-Sun is about speed; Round-the-Clock is about 24-hour coverage.

Chapter 7 considers radical strategies requiring a culture change. The first strategy implements a 24-hour organizational culture, the second strategy, Real-Time Simulated Co-location, timeshifts everyone to full overlap.

CHAPTER 5

Time Zone
Positioning Matters

Time Zone
Positioning Matters

Mikko was forming his project team, which was centered in Jyväskylä, Finland (GMT +2). For additional engineering staffing, the CTO gave Mikko a choice of working with the company's employees in Romania (GMT +2) or in Monterrey, Mexico (GMT -6). Mikko weighed the various trade-offs including time zones. He chose Mexico but decided to task that team with product testing since it required fewer daily conversations.

IKKO'S DECISION ILLUSTRATES the two key factors of this chapter—time zone location and the nature of the work. Many decision makers do not consider time zones when designing their distributed organization. Individuals, sub-teams, or divisions are determined based on availability, expertise, or a myriad of other reasons such as a recent merger. But, time zones are rarely considered. This is a mistake. Like the business adage, "location matters," it is clear that "time zones matter[54]" because the coordination costs are significant.

Yet some decision makers are paying attention. For example, some companies now issue RFPs, request for proposals, that specify in which time zone the work should be done. A specification such as "the work location has to be the U.S. East Coast, +/- 2" places nearly all of the Americas as eligible and disqualifies the Eastern Hemisphere as ineligible.

For time zone-related decision-making, one can choose locations that span the continuum—from full overlap, to some overlap, to far away. Each has its advantages and disadvantages. Before we get into location choice, though, it is essential to set the stage with task allocation and the nature of work.

Task Allocation:
Reduce Dependencies By Design

FROM A TIME ZONE PERSPECTIVE, many project teams are simply dealt their hand. Mikko from the above vignette could have received an order from his CTO: "You will work with seven employees in Mexico and three in Romania!" But, of course, Mikko had a choice.

On a project basis, once the project's staffing and configuration is set, the next crucial step is *task allocation*. Allocating complex tasks is best done by architecting modularity.[55] Modular design is usually preferred because it reduces complexity, thus reducing the coordination complexity. After all, it is this coordination complexity that is aggravated by time zone differences.

Modular design is a principle applied in collaborations every day, even in the kitchen: "You grill the meat, I'll make the side dishes." The distinct allocation of tasks, then, is a key success factor for most time zone-separated global collaboration. Attention to this principle ensures that each site has a significant task that relies as little as possible on other sites. By minimizing *dependence* between the sites, coordination costs are reduced.

Mikko made a choice from among the four squares of the time zone strategy matrix (fig. 5-0), balancing resources and tasks in order to minimize the task dependencies, handoffs, and possibilities for clarification requests.[56] As one global tech manager told us: "Managers prefer people in the same time zone, but it's not really resource-realistic."

Of course not all managers are content with the hand they are dealt. When coordination is too challenging between distant sites, project managers have been known to fly their key people from site A to site B for several weeks. This is common in technology firms, especially in R&D firms. Such ad-hoc time zone solutions, however, are quite expensive and tend to disappear during lean times.

Location Choice

MANAGERS MAKE CHOICES about global locations for factories, call centers, new hotels, employment expansion and other projects. A myriad of factors go into these decisions. When do time zones play a role?

Near

Where is the best location for collaborative work vis-à-vis time zones? The paramount parameter in answering this question is the *not*—not having to work/meet at uncomfortable hours at night. For example, after he switched from collaborating with Asia to collaborating with a location closer to home, an American manager confessed to us that, "it sure is nice not having to wake up at night for conference calls."

India and Brazil are midway locations. India's workday overlaps a geographical area that accounts for 73% of the world's GDP, the entire Eastern Hemisphere.[57] Brazil juts into the Atlantic Ocean between Europe and North America enabling its workday to overlap with both these continents (fig. 5-1). This is convenient for Brazil's technology companies. According to Brasscom, one of the country's technology associations, nearly 100% of Brazil's foreign IT partners have time zone overlap with Brazil.

During Brazil's winter

		4	3	2	1	Brazil	1	2	3	4	5
		U.S. Pacific	U.S. Mountain	U.S. Central	U.S. East Coast					London, Lisbon	Western Europe
		GMT -7		GMT-5	GMT-4	GMT -3				GMT +1	GMT +2

During Brazil's summer

6	5	4	3	2	1	Brazil	1	2	3	4	5
U.S. Pacific	U.S. Mountain	U.S. Central	U.S. East Coast					London, Lisbon	Western Europe		
GMT -8	GMT -7	GMT -6	GMT-5			GMT -2		GMT 0	GMT +1		

Figure 5-1: Brazil's time zone overlaps with its North American and European partners.

In a 2010 study we conducted with our colleague Rafael Prikladnicki,[58] we found that there was a great deal of sync communications in Brazilian–American IT collaborations with their large time overlap, just as we prescribed in previous chapters. The distant collaborators regularly used various awareness and communications technologies, particularly instant messaging and other chat tools, along with their various built-in awareness tools. As expected, we also found high usage of voice communications during overlap times. But even with the natural large overlap, we still found pervasive timeshifting to accommodate better collaboration.

Very Near: Nearshoring

"Just a few time zones away, managing an outsourcer
in Costa Rica can be relatively easy."
Businessweek 2009[59]

Nearshoring means sourcing service work to a foreign, lower-wage country that is relatively close in distance or time zone, or preferably both. In addition to being time zone proximate, the customer also expects to benefit from cultural, linguistic, economic, political, or historical linkages.

Thus, one often finds nearshore pairings such as the English-speaking Malta and Britain (one hour time difference), Colombia and Miami (no time zone difference), Morocco and France (one hour time difference), Estonia and Finland (no time zone difference) and the Chinese city of Dalian and Tokyo (no time zone difference). Taking this idea a step further, some American companies are "rural sourcing" to nearby small university towns where labor costs are much lower than those in the big cities.[60]

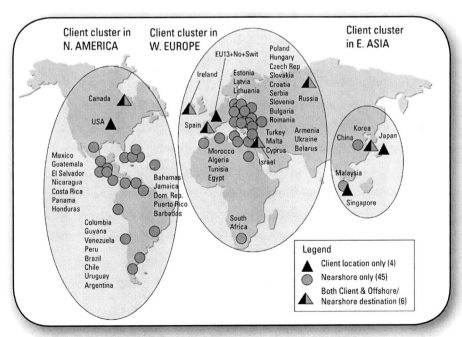

Figure 5-2: Nearshore clusters match clients, mostly in North America and Western Europe, with time zone proximate locations.

When the nearshoring wave began, we conducted a study with our colleague Pamela Abbott[61] and found that this phenomenon clustered around three continental time-zone bands (see map in fig. 5-2): one in the Americas (maximum span of seven hours), one centered around Western Europe (maximum span of three hours) and one in East Asia (maximum span of one hour).[62] One could also add smaller nearshore bands: one centered around Persian Gulf clients with suppliers on the subcontinent, and another centered around Australian clients. In 2005, the number of countries that positioned themselves as nearshore was already surprisingly high. The map indicates fifty-one nations with at least one company or association making the nearshore claim.

Very Near: SeaCode, the ultimate very near fantasy

This case is still just a story. It is a business dream of creative entrepreneurs who are versed in both maritime and global technology work. SeaCode is a company that aims to reengineer nearshoring by modifying aging cruise ships to house software programmers, and then anchoring these ships in international waters surrounding the United States and Europe. The first ship was going to be permanently stationed three miles out to sea, off the San Diego coastline (not a bad place since San Diego is considered by many to have the best weather in the United States). The ship would be a floating software factory for programmers working for California-based firms. Clients could even visit for meetings by boat or helicopter. The SeaCode founders envisioned working conditions for programmers to be quite pleasant: food and housing provided along with free laundry and medical services. Given that programmers would have "seaman" status, they would be able to visit onshore. Since they would live and work at sea, the programmers would not need the costly and controversial H1B U.S. temporary work visas.

The controversial SeaCode venture has never set sail and seems unlikely to, but its creativity embodies the primacy of time zones. It seems more convivial to work in California during daylight hours than to do significant timeshifting between Asia and the U.S. West Coast.

Warning: Northern–Southern Hemispheres may shift the best location

Southern Hemisphere locations may confuse the decision-making around location choice because their effective time separation varies rather substantially by season. Due to opposing

DSTs phasing in and out in both the North and South, some pairs of collaborators shift two hours between winter and summer. An example is a Sao Paulo–California dyad. In this situation, a four-hour time difference changes to a six-hour time difference during the Brazilian summer. A six-hour time separation affects the nature of collaboration according to one Brazilian manager working with California: "[that this type of collaboration requires] mind-set changing when it moves back two hours." Note that not all key locations use DST in the Southern Hemisphere: Brazil, Chile, Sydney, and Auckland use it, but Buenos Aires and South Africa do not.

Very far

Much of this chapter has focused on working in proximate time zones. But being far apart can be advantageous too. In the next chapters we introduce Follow-the-Sun and Round-the-Clock strategies. Both involve locations that are far apart, often as far apart as possible (having a twelve-hour difference between them). In such cases, setting up locations in different hemispheres is done by design in order to attain either speed, for Follow-the-Sun, or 24-hour coverage, for Round-the-Clock.

India emerged in the 1990s as a destination mostly for faraway American clients. Since then, India's industry and individuals began to embrace the narrative of distant time zones, a narrative that has contributed to its ascent in the world of offshore outsourcing. As early as 1996, a journalist for the technology magazine *Computerworld* was writing about this Follow-the-Sun/24-hour coverage narrative in an article titled "Seven by Twenty-Four."[63]

Rule of Two

Wary of complicated far-flung teams, some companies have instituted an informal rule: *The Rule of Two*. The Rule of Two states that a maximum of two time zones are represented in a distributed project team. This is an informal rule of course. We have heard of this notion from employees at Dell, Intel, and other large firms.

This Rule of Two is clearly an outcome of collective learning, pain, and frustration resulting from those many idealistic far-flung projects of the early 2000s. For example, we learned that at one large American tech company, projects were allocated to teams and sites based on where team members were located, even across multiple time zones. But the company learned that multiple time zone-allocations have high coordination costs, so the company instead concentrated its resources in geographic "centers of excellence." The company decided not to have more than two sites working on the same project.

Time Zone as a Calling Card

NATIONS COMPETE, and now they compete in their time zone position. Since the new millennium, it has also become fashionable to position national competitive advantage in terms of time zone. In 2009, New Zealand began a public discussion of such positioning. Its strategists declared that the nation's time zone makes it an ideal location as a global financial hub since New Zealand is just west of the International Date Line and every financial day begins in New Zealand. Along the same lines, India's IT industry has long positioned itself as operating in an ideal time zone geography: *we get the work done while you're sleeping!* The positioning was very much focused on its dominant early customers, the Americans, nine or more time zones away. In fact, the time zone position has become such a pervasive narrative in India that we found the entire tech industry embracing this narrative as one of the essential strengths of Indian IT.[64] Just ask any young Indian knowledge worker why India is so successful, and we promise that time zone will be one of the factors in most answers you receive.

1. Strong domestic IT
2. Cultural similarity to the United States
3. Geographic proximity
4. **Time zone compatibility**
5. Geopolitical stability
6. Creative power of Brazilian engineers
7. Areas of excellence: banking, healthcare, e-gov

Figure 5-3: Apex-Brazil's seven dimensions of national IT branding, circa 2005[65]
(emphasis added by authors). Apex-Brazil is the Brazilian Trade and Investment Promotion Agency.

As a reaction to this, the Brazilian IT industry began to promote time zone proximity in order to differentiate itself from the Indian IT industry. The sector's message is: *You can easily work with us because whenever you want to reach us, we're working while you're working.* The various Brazilian national associations have tended to promote Brazil's time zone location as advantageous. Apex, a national agency, highlights time zone advantages (see fig. 7-3). We examined the time zone branding at Brazilian companies[66] and found that in an effort to differentiate themselves from other companies, 38% of them boast about their time zone location in their marketing literature.[67]

Time zone positioning also changes when a company gains national power. For example, Indian firms have stressed their time zone location for years. But now, as leading Indian tech services providers have become global giants and highly mature organizations in terms of technical capabilities, they have reduced the stress on India's time zone position. Now that the Indian giants have dozens of locations all over the world, they emphasize "coverage" and "24/7."

The positioning of companies has different attributes depending on their time zone. Firms that stress their time zones' proximity are selling compatibility, comfort, and convenience. Those that stress their time zones' distance are selling speed and efficiency.

Time Zone location hype from nations and companies
(emphasis added by authors)

❝ India had flourished not because of any tax advantage, but because of its cost and quality advantage, its huge, young labour market and its **time zone** and demographic advantage. ❞
Times of India, 2010

❝ **Time zone** advantages were part of nearly every pitch I heard from an outsourcer; think of it as an extension of the 'nearshore' philosophy. It's why the representatives of the in-the-works Dubai Outsource Zone were touting that idea's advantages for a wide range of enterprises (it's smack in the Middle East and only 4-5 hours from key European and Asian markets, you see). It's also why players from Argentina and Mexico were touting their advantages for the North American market; an Argentina or a Brazil may be in the Southern Hemisphere and Mexico is far enough away for many businesses, but on the clock, they're only an hour off of many North American businesses, if that. ❞
From CIO pipeline, an IT periodical, 2004

continued...

“ *We have a time zone advantage – we are GMT +1.* ”
An Italian CEO overheard boasting, 2008

“ *Time Saving: Our offshore services exploit **time zone** differences by practical deployment of extra shifts for faster time-to-market.* ”
Ness Technologies' offshore provider website, 2008

“ *Africa is known as a promising economic area in all business fields, including outsourcing due to the reduced labor costs and the benefit of having a European **time zone.*** ”
Business South Africa, 2010

“ *We do this because Capgemini supports much of its consulting efforts around the globe with a huge workforce in India. These are the people that **work while you sleep** and handle the more technical aspects of the work stream.* ”
Capgemini blog 2010

“ *Why Camp6: We help you extend your office by enabling you to add team members without taking them on your payroll and by extending your operation to 24 hours –* **we work while you sleep!** ”
Camp6, an accounting BPO firm based in India, website, 2011

“ *Our development center is located just one time zone east of New York. This geographical proximity translates into easier access, better communication and lower costs. Brazil is conveniently located in a time zone between North America and Europe. With minor shifts, we can maximize the number of hours in which both our teams and our clients are at work.* ”
Paradigma Internet, a Brazilian IT firm, 2010

“ *So, while wages might be high [for news editing] – possibly even generally higher in Australia than in the UK, by shifting work from night shifts to day, money can be saved. In this way, **Australia's time zone becomes a competitive advantage.*** ”
Can Oz compete in the outsourcing market? Tim Worstall, The Register, 2011

ACTIONABLE ITEMS

- **Time zones are at the table.** Any collaboration decision in your organization must use time zones as part of the decision evaluation—whether the decision is about an internal team, an outsourcer, working with a client, or your role in a global supply chain.

- **Near.** Actively seek locations that are time zone proximate. This applies to most collaboration cases, but not to all.

- **Simplify.** Take complex time zone configurations and reduce the number of time zones. This applies to most collaboration cases, but not to all.

- **Modularize.** If you are handed a set configuration across time zones, then actively reduce dependencies between locations.

- **Compete.** Time zones can be a source of competitive advantage. Use them.

CHAPTER 6

Follow-The-Sun
and Round-The-Clock

Follow-The-Sun and Round-The-Clock

In early 1997, just a few years after the commercial Internet took off, IBM CEO Lou Gerstner trumpeted a work innovation: IBM's ability to do Follow-the-Sun software development. This was probably the earliest instance of a Follow-the-Sun project in the software world. Gerstner described an audacious global software team that IBM had just launched: a five-team, five-country development project.[68] The work cycle began with the U.S. team who would set up a work specification for each small software module. The Americans would send it off at the end of their day. The other four teams, all in the Eastern Hemisphere, would turn those specifications into program code and at the end of their day ship the code back to the United States ready for successive rounds of reviews and feedback.

AS THIS LANDMARK PROJECT illustrates, time zone differences can be an advantage. *Follow-the-Sun* and *Round-the-Clock* are two strategies that take advantage of time zone differences, and these have become the great seductions of global work in that while you sleep, others are working and getting the job done. It is a perfect symmetry that every listener falls in love with. When American shift workers go home for the evening, Asian shift workers are just getting started, and when the earth turns another half a revolution, the two sites trade places once again.

Yet, there are two strands to this time zone strategy that are actually remarkably *different*. The first is Follow-the-Sun work—unfinished work that is handed off to the next site on a daily basis. The second is Round-the-Clock work, which includes global help desks, global support centers, global trading desks, and more. As we open this chapter, we make a sharp distinction between these two types of time zone strategies:

- Follow-the-Sun is about *speed*.
- Round-the-Clock is about 24-hour *coverage*.

Yes, both of these approaches leverage time zone separation, but for very different purposes and with very different types of tasks and coordination challenges. Recall from the time zone strategy matrix (fig. 5-0 in the introduction to Section II) that what separates these two strategies is the nature of the work dependency. The sites in Follow-the-Sun are very dependent on one another because they are coupled, while the sites in Round-the-Clock are not.

An example of a Follow-the-Sun task is rapid prototyping, which is a creative, constructive task with serious coordination challenges as described in the following passage about a California tech company working with Asia.

> **❝** *Communication among NetDevices colleagues, more complicated than mere cubicle chatter, is carefully choreographed to avoid workflow hiccups that can cause days of delay. There is the critical nightly handoff of software code-in-progress to engineers across the Pacific Ocean. Quick cell phone conversations at all hours. Weekend e-mail exchanges.* **❞**
> **Siliconweek**[69]

In contrast, Round-the-Clock work includes the familiar helpdesk or Tier 1 support (Tier 1 is similar to helpdesk, but often for more technical queries). A helpdesk, unlike a full project, handles a task quickly, often in just a few minutes, so there is little dependency between the distant sites. The kind of tasks that helpdesks take care of are said to be *granular*. In other words, they are very small like a grain of sand. Thus, there is little coordination challenge in handing-off work between various global sites.

Regrettably, there is no consensus in the marketplace of tech jargon about the meaning of the terms Follow-the-Sun and Round-the-Clock. Both terms are used loosely. The marketers have subjugated the terms and diluted them of much of their meaning. We hope this book will change that.

Follow-the-Sun

FOLLOW-THE-SUN[70] is an intuitive concept: handoff work from one site to the next, in shifts. Consequently, the company can theoretically reduce the project duration by 50% if two shifts are involved; or if there are three sites working three sequential shifts, duration could be theoretically reduced by 67%. [71]

The earliest Follow-the-Sun project at IBM

In the opening of this chapter, we began telling the story of IBM's early Follow-the-Sun project.[72] IBM's managers were quite daring. Not only were they working in Follow-the-Sun, they had also created an unusual organizational structure and were experimenting with new software. IBM set up four equal-sized teams in four low-cost, offshore, labor sites. The hub was in Seattle, and the other sites were located in Beijing; Bangalore, India; Minsk, Belarus; and Riga, Latvia.

Each team had exactly thirty-one professionals. IBM called this structure the *Phalanx*. At each of the four sites there were five people in each of the core specialist areas such as graphics and technical writing. Part of the original vision was to create a reusable team structure so that IBM could reuse it to expand to other sites around the world. Another reason was that the structure made it easy to communicate across sites. Every person always knew whom to contact since each site had the very same organizational logic.

And, on top of that, this global team was also developing a progressive-type of software architecture. Rather than developing one large product as was customary, the undertaking was to develop many small components, known as Javabeans, where each software bean could be developed rapidly.

For IBM, Follow-the-Sun did not work. As it turned out, a daily turnaround (pure Follow-the-Sun) was too ambitious for both sides—the Asian/European software coders and their American reviewers. It was too much to digest in one day's work. A cycle of every two or three days was more doable, so the project settled into a rhythm of two "code drops" per week from each location. In the meantime, the U.S. site had assigned about half a dozen software beans to each offshore site. For example, while the Beijing team was waiting for review and feedback on one software bean, it was simultaneously working on other beans. At steady state, the IBM project was juggling about twenty beans between the hub and the remote sites. However, soon the Seattle hub became a bottleneck. It was handling too many demanding, complicated tasks.

After a few months, the project managers threw up their hands and began managing this global project using conventional global approaches, either parallel or phase-based. Looking back, the project manager said, "Recognizing that time zones are a problem [instead of an advantage] is the first step in managing it." The project got so far off its original shift design that the teams from Latvia and Belarus practiced "Follow-the-Moon" as it was jokingly referred to. These sites were pushing hard and working eighteen-hour days. Clearly, this was not what was envisioned in Follow-the-Sun. This seductive approach was too difficult to follow.

Time-to-Market

Follow-the-Sun is all about speed, or more precisely, about reducing the calendar duration of a project: for example, reducing a nine-month project to one that would run for only six months. The related business concept is called *time-to-market*, the length of time it takes from product conception until the product is available for use or sale[73] (fig. 6-1). Time-to-market is most important in industries where products become outmoded quickly, such as mobile telephone handsets and mobile software.

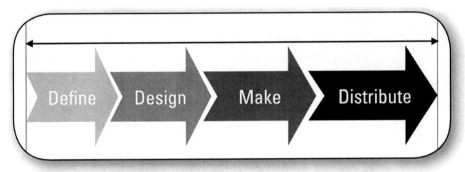

Figure 6-1. Follow-the-Sun has the potential to reduce Time-to-Market.

Working in shifts over more hours of the day, or more days of the week, produces more output. As a result, Follow-the-Sun is a case of better *calendar efficiency,* which is the percent of all calendar time that is used productively for work.[74] A traditional forty-hour workweek uses only a small fraction of the calendar, just 23.8% of the week (40/168). At that level there is a lot of room for calendar efficiency improvement. Working two shifts increases calendar efficiency to almost 50% of the week. The second shift can be located anywhere in the world in order to increase calendar efficiency. Time zone leverage kicks in when the shift workers are assigned to a shift that most people in the world prefer— daytime.

Speed and delay across time zones

We have been intrigued by speed, duration reduction, and delays in global work. In our own research stream, we studied the effects of time separation on speed. With our colleagues, Jonathon Cummings and Cindy Pickering,[75] we studied global teams at Intel and found that the time zone difference between two technical project team members increased delay, but this increase was only statistically significant when team members had no overlapping work time. In other words, there was a threshold of separation above which there was a delay (a nine-hour difference in our study).

We also found impacts on speed (productivity) across time zones, but in the other direction! In our laboratory experiment study with Ning Nan,[76] we found that as time separation increased, so did speed, but at the expense of the quality of the task. Restated, we found a tradeoff between speed and quality. Why, then, the contradiction from our previous study at Intel? With a somewhat granular task, the student subjects in the experiments benefited from the lack of interruptions due to time separation, which led to the increase in speed, but this came at the expense of lower quality. At Intel, the engineers worked on complex and uncertain projects. While they may have benefited from quiet time and got more done this way, our interpretation is that they had to devote extra time to deliver quality work due to communication problems; and this wiped out the speed advantage.

The challenge of the perfect handoff

Most knowledge work collaboration, such as software projects, uses configurations that are either parallel (fig. 6-2a) or by phase (fig. 6-2b). These configurations are nice and lean in that they minimize dependencies and handoffs. Recall that in chapter 3 we devoted a lot of ink to handoffs because they are difficult.

In the simple examples pictured in figure 6-2, there is one handoff point per project for the parallel approach, integration at the end, and two handoff points per project for the phase approach. All these small numbers are in contrast to *three per day* for a Follow-the-Sun, totaling to hundreds (!) for a typical project duration. Each coordination relay, like the passing of the baton in an Olympic relay race, has to be near perfect, with as few coordination glitches as possible. Notice that global projects that use parallel or phase approaches are *not* leveraging time zones in any way; they just happen to be employing workers spread out across the globe. While these three examples ignore the relative size of each team, it is clear that given the lopsided large number of handoffs in Follow-the-Sun, its coordination efforts are likely to be high.

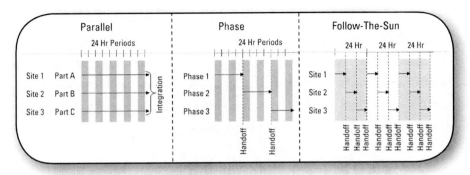

Figure 6-2. Follow-the-Sun compared to other globally distributed configurations.
We refer to parallel and phase-based as "conventional global configurations."

The myth of Follow-the-Sun

❝ *The sun never sets on the British empire.* **❞**

**Adage about the British empire
at the peak of its power in the 1800s.**

Both the British adage and the 1990s IBM Follow-the-Sun story earlier in this chapter exemplify a similar fascination. Encircling the globe still captures the imagination.

Yet, there have been relatively few successful cases of Follow-the-Sun. It is simply too hard to do for the entire duration of a project. Many have claimed successful Follow-the-Sun projects but, on closer inspection, while these projects were indeed globally dispersed and were indeed being worked on close to twenty-four hours a day, project workers did *not* practice the daily handoff routine of Follow-the-Sun as we have defined it more rigorously. So, while the projects may have been successful, *they did not leverage time zones in any way.*

Just like the IBM case before it, CLX, an American software firm tried Follow-the-Sun for software application development. "Yes, we did development onshore [in the United States] and testing offshore [in India] at night," said the Vice President of Engineering with a long sigh; however, he conceded, "[it was difficult and] I don't advocate this work style."

We actively searched for Follow-the-Sun projects over the years. For example, we conducted a study at one of the giants of the Indian software industry, Infosys, at its famous and beautiful campus in Bangalore. We sought out software projects that may have been using Follow-the-Sun, but couldn't find any. To the contrary, we discovered that in most projects there were challenges of coordination and small delays due to time zone differences. Contrary to the myth, Indian firms situated far from their clients in the United States rarely, if ever, use Follow-the-Sun.[77] Rather, India-based software engineers work hard to overcome time zone challenges. Workers stay late and devote special attention to highly async-structured processes. While there isn't much interest in Follow-the-Sun, some Indian firms leverage Round-the-Clock, which we describe later in this chapter.

What is needed for Follow-the-Sun to work

Follow-the-Sun, because of its built-in dependencies across time zones, requires formidable daily handoff coordination, which is very much at the heart of its difficulty. This approach has been manageable in many firms for short bursts of collaboration such as the prototyping period of a software project. However, for a full project, the coordination demands are daunting. Nevertheless, if Follow-the-Sun is to be achieved successfully, here are the three practices we believe are vital:

1. Use highly structured processes. All the project's members and managers have to subscribe to a culture that is highly structured, including a culture of daily documentation and careful status reporting.
2. Manage handoffs effectively. The verbal handoff during the fixed daily overlap period is essential. For some global configurations, this would require a small timeshift.
3. Make use of special tools. Special customized tools have to be woven together or mashed-up.

Structure

In the world of software, a highly structured process is often referred to as a methodology. Those who have examined Follow-the-Sun recognize the importance of selecting the right software development methodology that spans the entire development process and supports the special needs of daily handoffs. IBM tried this with its Phalanx in the 1990s; similarly, EDS, now HP, crafted a special methodological adaptation for Follow-the-Sun.[78] Both didn't get far.

We believe that the most promising methodology to attain Follow-the-Sun is the *"agile"* approach. We see three reasons for this. First, agile uses short, *"time boxed"*[79] iterations—i.e., short phases with strict deadlines. Features go through the entire cycle: they are designed, tested, developed and presented. Second, agile enables granular and structured daily handoffs because activities are intertwined. For example, it is common when using the agile approach to keep the integration *green*, the color-code for indicating that all tests have passed inspection, at the end of the workday, thereby ensuring high quality handoffs. Third, agile inspires a sustainable pace that fits the goal of working mostly during one's daylight hours.

Lessons from our study

As part of our research with our colleague Yael Dubinsky[80] and her software engineering students at the Israel Institute of Technology, we built special tools for distributed teams working in Follow-the-Sun mode. The tool was built as a plug-in to Eclipse, IBM's open integrated development platform. Dubinsky named the tool "baton" to emphasize the centrality of the handoff.

With Dubinsky, we also began to examine the challenge of Follow-the-Sun and to evaluate it against traditional distributed software work.[81] To do this, we conducted two exploratory comparative field studies. Our study used student teams engaged in agile development, divided into Follow-the-Sun teams and control teams. While the control teams could coordinate in any way they wished, including face-to-face and synchronous, the Follow-the-Sun teams, in order to simulate time zone differences, had strict rules imposed on their interaction. The study task required four hundred person hours per team.

In this comparison study, we found that Follow-the-Sun teams performed equal to or better than the control teams on functionality and level of quality. More importantly, using our rough proxies for duration reduction, the Follow-the-Sun teams achieved shorter duration as compared to their respective control teams (10% and 50% reduction in the two comparisons). These results suggest some promise for Follow-the-Sun with short agile iterations.

Other data revealed an unexpected finding: the daily time pressure imposed on the Follow-the-Sun teams compelled participants to work more productively. This is notable because our implicit assumption was that each site has equal productivity and the challenge would be in managing the coordination overhead between the sites. But, as we learned in this study, the Follow-the-Sun participants produced more per hour individually. We think this stems from *time-boxing*. Time-boxing impacts the individual behavior of a programmer by setting strict deadlines for each work iteration, resulting in greater focus. Personal time-boxing curbs perfectionist tendencies, procrastination, and prevents an individual from overcommitting to a task. Separately, we also found that the Follow-the-Sun teams produced more and better documentation.

In summary, our small-scale study represents a proof-of-concept that Follow-the-Sun for software is viable. But this is possible only when the team adopts a work procedure like the agile approach, which is designed for very rapid daily iterations. Using this approach, at the end of the workday the work output is packaged and finished to be handed-off to the next site.

A different Follow-the-Sun: back office operations

We end the section with Follow-the-Sun for business processes. It is nicely illustrated in the mortgage lifecycle process diagramed by Sutherland Global Services (fig. 6-3). Sutherland, a U.S.-based firm, is one of the largest business process outsourcing firms with many large corporate clients, especially in North America. Its mortgage lifecycle process is decomposed into twelve steps, only five of which have to be done in the front office. This implies that only these five steps need to be done in the United States by American employees. These front office steps typically require local knowledge, or local contact of some kind. All the other seven steps can be sliced off and tasked to the back office, usually in the Philippines or India. Anything in the back office tends to be less expensive.

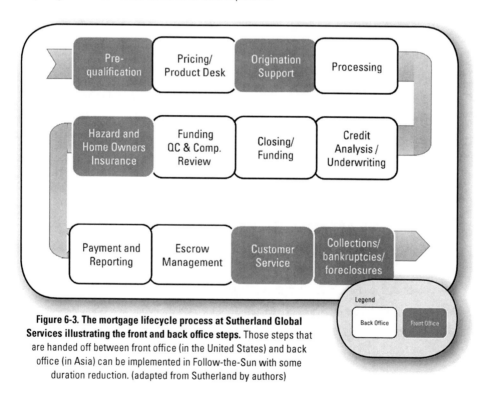

Figure 6-3. The mortgage lifecycle process at Sutherland Global Services illustrating the front and back office steps. Those steps that are handed off between front office (in the United States) and back office (in Asia) can be implemented in Follow-the-Sun with some duration reduction. (adapted from Sutherland by authors)

More importantly, from our perspective, since there are alternating steps in the mortgage lifecycle process, then work can be accelerated (for example, handoff between the first step, pre-qualification, and the second step, pricing/product desk). Typically Americans work during their daylight hours on the front office tasks and pass the file on to Asian centers that work during their daylight hours on the back office tasks. Organizations like Sutherland have invested a great deal of knowledge in engineering the steps in order to optimize both cost and duration. This careful engineering of the document workflow is what separates mortgage loan origination from the messy life cycle of software development, which was described earlier in this chapter. The mortgage process is highly structured while the software process is not, at least by comparison. Using the more theoretical terms that we introduce later in chapter 10, more structured and predictable processes can be coordinated "mechanistically."

Round-the-Clock

ROUND-THE-CLOCK is a type of workflow strategy that leverages time zones to achieve 24-hour *coverage*. This global scheduling model is somewhat like that of the local 24/7 supermarket that needs to staff the store efficiently. At the 24-hour supermarket, different shifts do roughly similar work but at different times of the day. The Round-the-Clock model is similar—i.e., call centers all over the world are staffed to answer calls. The benefit is 24-hour coverage, with all shifts working during daylight hours. In these operations, the goal of leveraging time zone separation is continuous service.

The incoming calls are routed by specialized software to the next available person or to the designated center in, say, Makati, Philippines or in Omaha, United States.[82] Some of the transfer may be done automatically in the Cisco switch. Sometimes, one hears a tiny "hoo-hoo" noise during the transfer, which comes from the call being passed-on from one switch to another.

A key difference between Follow-the-Sun and Round-the-Clock is the *duration of a transaction*. While Follow-the-Sun deals with ongoing unfinished tasks, Round-the-Clock usually deals with highly granular transactions that typically take just a few minutes to complete. Within the industry this duration is called average *handle time*, and it is a key productivity measure. Here are some actual data from one provider. At client A, a large American transportation company, the average handle time is four minutes; at client B, an Internet service provider where technical support is needed, the average handle time is twenty minutes. While these handle times are dramatically different (handle time at client B takes five times longer), both are still much shorter than a typical work shift. There are few client queries that need to be handed off to the next shift. That is, the work is decoupled between the distant sites—there are no dependencies.

CASE STUDY
Dell's database operations

A typical Round-the-Clock operation is the case of Dell's database operations. Dell, the giant technology and services company, has two offshore units that do Round-the-Clock support on all the company's database operations. One is in Porto Alegre (GMT -3) in Brazil and the other in Cyberjaya in Malaysia (GMT +8), half a world away. Each location is responsible for a twelve-hour shift.

The Brazilian–Malaysian pairing was not the original configuration. At first, Malaysia was charged with 24-hour coverage using two shifts. The workers would switch shifts periodically. Each would do a shift for two months and then switch. So, all workers were working the night shift half the year. Dissatisfaction resulted and many workers left. Therefore, Dell decided to do Round-the-Clock with a different location. Since it already had a large center in Porto Alegre, Brazil seemed like the right choice.

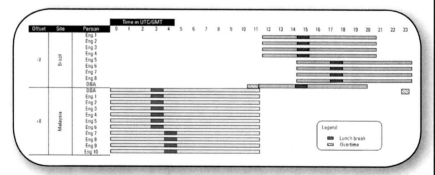

Figure 6-4. Dell's support centers in Brazil (GMT -3) and Malaysia (GMT+8) hand off work every day after a twelve-hour shift.

continued...

Internally, shifts are designed according to local preferences. The Malaysians like working 12-hour shifts and then having three days off. The Brazilians are somewhat restricted due to labor laws, so they work staggered shifts of 8.8 to 10 hours (the standard Brazilian workday is 8.8 hours).

Each of two locations has eight to ten full-time database engineers. Operations involve receiving and fixing problems that appear on "tickets." Some tickets come from humans, while 90% are generated from automated machines.

The key people are the DataBase Administrators (DBAs). The DBAs do a short handoff at the transition of each shift. The handoff is short in this kind of work because the DBAs are experienced at handling many tickets, and the processes have become well oiled, mature, and stable. Moreover, there is relatively little to hand off between shifts since the vast majority of the several hundred tickets per shift are closed within minutes of their receipt.

The handoff itself is both verbal and written. The written portion is fairly straightforward and covers a log that includes the handful of open active issues. The verbal portion of the handoff is usually about fifteen minutes long, which ritually ends with "have a nice shift!"

Other Round-the-Clock models

Round-the-Clock is widespread and varied, so we present two more examples for Round-the-Clock work, the first at a large American bank and the second, for testing, through the microsourcer uTest.com.

As opposed to Dell's two locations, Maryland Bank's Round-the-Clock work is far-flung. Maryland Bank's Tier 3 IT support is targeted at only the critically difficult bugs—those that cannot be addressed by Tier 1 and Tier 2. For this vital operation, the bank designed Round-the-Clock coverage by splitting the work between its internal global staff and the global staff of its outsourcing provider LGG (both Maryland Bank and LGG are aliases). The combined staff is scattered around four nations and many more locations: forty in India, three in Britain, three in U.S. East Coast, three in U.S. West Coast, and one in New Zealand.

When a defect comes into Tier 3 support, the responsibility matrix allocates it to the most suitable person or the available person in one of the four nations. Most of the staff at the Delhi location in India has two overlapping shifts, early and late. The early shift comes into work at 07:00. The later shift comes in to work at 13:00. This is convenient to both shifts because heavy traffic commute times are avoided. There are occasional handoffs between the locations: The India center will sometimes handoff a difficult defect to the American experts many time zones away for background task research during their workday and then it will be passed back to India.

A very different approach, also leveraging time zones, is at uTest.[83] This company offers Round-the-Clock coverage using a novel work shift design in which uTest is a middleman, akin to an eBay, but for 24/7 software testers as individual contractors. For example, a large global firm contracts for 24-hour testing services where the demand for this service fluctuates quite a bit during the day. uTest taps into its large global supply of software testers, many of them working from home, and has them ready for work at shifts that are convenient to both parties.

The myth of Round-the-Clock

Round-the-Clock, like its cousin Follow-the-Sun, is sometimes used as a slogan when there is really no leverage of time zones for better coverage. Such is the case of the American company that we shall call RemCo. We begin by explaining RemCo's global shift design and then we explore where the myth comes in.

RemCo is a large firm in the consumer electronic products business. It offers its customers 24/7 Tier 1 support during which customers call in with problems and questions. It needs to staff this service 168 hours per week (24x7). It splits the shifts between its internal RemCo employees and its outsourcing provider KyleSystems in India (both RemCo and KyleSystems are aliases).

RemCo provides support twenty-four hours a day, Monday through Friday, from its own internal centers using shiftwork in the United States. It outsources to KyleSystems just for weekend work, for 54 hours on Saturday-Sunday. Thus, the interval is for coverage from Friday midnight in America (00:00 GMT -5) until Monday morning (06:00 GMT -5). KyleSystems provides support from India, so for its employees, work time is between Saturday at 10:30 (GMT+5:30) and Monday at 16:30. In India, KyleSystems has designed shifts that are nine hours long, eight work hours plus one hour for lunch. Managers and supervisors tend to work longer. But the workload is not spread out evenly because most of RemCo's callers need help during American daylight time, so most of the Indian employees work evening and night shifts, and only a minority work during the day.

The foregoing were the details. The facts, if you will. And now we come to the myth. The KyleSystems manager adamantly claims that his firm is tapping into the power of time zone differences: Round-the-Clock and Follow-the-Sun. We were surprised by the inconsistency between the facts and the myth, but then again, the myth of time zones in global work is very powerful and hard to shake off. As with nearly all firms that provide global support, for the KyleSystems manager these constructs are part of his reflexive lexicon, even though in the RemCo-KyleSystems partnership there is no shift design that uses time zone advantage.

Rather, RemCo via KyleSystems is leveraging inexpensive offshore labor in the Indian call centers to cover unpopular shifts. It is a way for American clients, such as RemCo, to avoid imposing expensive off-hours on their American work force. In this way, it preserves some work-life balance for the Americans.

The myth of Round-the-Clock has two opposing narratives for Asian workers. The first, an unfavorable one, is that this is just time zone colonialism. The wealthy nations are now colonizing nations via time zones. For example, one academic critic, Kiran Mirchandani,[84] writes, "... call centre workers live and work in India, but are required to organize their lives in terms of American times, celebrations, and communication styles."

The second narrative is the pulsating excitement of a new class of upwardly mobile young workers. The night shift can be exciting, especially when one is young and paid extra. The Call Center Avenue of metro Manila is Emerald Avenue in Pasig City. One hundred call centers are located along a short strip of tall office buildings. Most employees come to work after 18:00 in order to answer calls during the North American daylight hours. With all these young workers working 24/7, the avenue has a wide range of restaurants open at all hours. And, every Friday night at midnight, when the call centers are full, the busy avenue is closed to traffic and there's a *banchetto*, a lavish street feast and party.

ACTIONABLE ITEMS

- **Experiment.** Since Follow-the-Sun is rather difficult, experiment with it first for short phases of a project cycle. It is better to have successful experiences with discrete and small parts of a project, which can accelerate learning.
- **Perfect the handoff process with Follow-the-Sun.** Daily handoffs need to be routinized and structured with both written and verbal components. For some global configurations, this requires a small timeshift.
- **Structured process.** Follow-the-Sun requires a highly structured process. All the project members have to buy into this culture, including the daily routine of documentation and careful status reporting.
- **Build the tool.** Special customized tools have to be mashed-up for Follow-the-Sun.
- **Reengineer process.** In order to achieve Round-the-Clock work, reengineer and decouple the process steps so that each step can be accomplished independently and completely.

CHAPTER 7

Two Radical Options

Two Radical Options

THE STRATEGIES in the previous chapter *leverage* time zone differences, whereas the radical strategies here *mitigate* time zones differences while relying on moderate to heavy timeshifting. We pronounce these strategies as "radical" because both are premised on organizational culture creation, which is always hard to do. The first radical strategy ruptures the 20th century work conventions by creating a 24-hour culture that is more demanding, yet more flexible at the same time. The second radical strategy uses technology to create radical co-location. We learned about each of these strategies from our global visits.

Radical Strategy #1: Establish a 24-Hour Culture When Far Flung

A *24-HOUR CULTURE is a pact between the knowledge worker and the company in which the worker is flexible in his/her schedule in exchange for the company's schedule flexibility and a range of incentives and perks.* This delicate pact includes a psychological contract and a power imbalance. We will unpack these two a bit later.

Certainly, elements of a 24-hour organizational culture are already diffused. The scattertime that we described in chapter 1 is a type of 24-hour culture. Moreover, it can seem as if every company's slogan these days is "we are a global 24/7 firm." That said, the concept of a 24-hour culture we describe here is more than scattertime and more than slogans. To begin, we take you to India.

Two giant companies

Infosys, the giant Indian IT services company, now has a large, comfortable campus on the outskirts of Bangalore covering thirty hectares. At the center of the campus is the striking global conferencing building, resembling a space-center, which is often shown in documentaries to exemplify modern India. Let us take you back to 2005 when we first encountered its 24-hour culture.[85] Infosys was already an enormously successful company and was considered a highly desirable place to work, among India's best, receiving several awards as "best employer" from Hewitt Associates. It was also the first Indian firm to offer stock options to all qualified employees.

The large Infosys campuses in India are 24-hour campuses. At that time, most of the company's business was in the United States, meaning that, depending on season and U.S. location, its clients were 9.5 to 11.5 hours away. Someone had to timeshift, and it wasn't going to be the paying American client. Consequently, some of the 14,000 Infosys software engineers stayed late, worked overtime, or even worked overnight. In India-speak, this is called "stay back." The company provides amenities—open cafeterias and a well-equipped recreation center—for those who stay late. The campus is secure. Transportation home, on buses, is provided until 21:00.

In contrast to the Infosys culture, we visited the SAP global headquarters campus in Waldorf, Germany and found hardly any signs of a 24-hour culture. SAP is the largest European software company and a dominant force in enterprise systems. The massive SAP campus is no less impressive than the Infosys campus in Bangalore. It is a small city with its own bus stops and access roads, but SAP's lack of 24-hour culture had some employees griping. They recognized they were in a global technology company and needed to timeshift, stay late at work or work on weekends. But the company culture did not support this very well. For example, even though there were fabulous kitchens on each floor packed with coffee and goodies, there was no organized food after traditional work hours, so those who stayed late had to resort to ordering takeout.

In fact, food and transportation are important in the 24-hour culture. In addition, the employee transportation needs may actually dictate shift design.[86] The better-run Asian-based tech firms, for example, are mindful of these factors and usually provide free or discounted food and transport for evening shift workers[87]

Let's go back now to the pact. We stated previously that the 24-hour culture is a pact between employee and company. We begin first with the employee. The employee's commitments and obligations are in timeshifting, sometimes ad hoc. The employee offers flexibility regarding scheduling for the global meetings and collaborations as well as the overtime and weekend work. If an employee works primarily at the office, then he or she accepts that there are expectations of scattertime, with some required work from home. Essentially, the company commissions the ability to change work hours, and the employee has qualified control over his/her own schedule and may not have to physically commute to the office.

The company's commitments and obligations to this pact are shown first and foremost as being accommodating on hours and shifts and by eliminating a requirement to punch a clock.

Instead employees are assessed by production, output, and success measures. The second commitment for some workers is in the form of generous accommodations relating to on-site childcare, child-minders at home, or even elderly care for those with older family members at home. The third is in the form of perks. Food is always important: in-house extended food hours, in-house gourmet coffee, or whatever else that is indulgent. Other on-site facilities that a company needs to provide are beds for napping, or even sleeping, and perhaps exercise facilities and game rooms. The company also needs to be generous with transportation, offering special buses and taxis. Finally, the company needs to do what is necessary to make employees feel safe in getting to and from work at night.

The pact

Let's step back to examine what this pact means at a deeper level. An organizational culture that rests on this kind of pact has to be rooted in a common set of beliefs to support key company objectives. For example, Infosys in India needed to be responsive to its North American clients from the other side of the world. Infosys achieved this by communicating to employees the importance of working flexible hours and by conveying that those who did this were valued employees. And of course, the employees had to subscribe to these beliefs and goals. They had to believe that the goal of accommodating a client in a different time zone was as critically important as the company claimed it was.[88]

The 24-hour culture is easier to develop and maintain when the physical office is less important as in the case of a "virtual company." For example, in 2011 we visited small virtual web applications firms in Vietnam and the Philippines. Employees at these companies tended to work at all hours, especially at night, in order to be responsive to their clients in North America.

Some companies try to take advantage of the employer-employee power imbalance by demanding 24-hour obligations without delivering on their side of the implicit pact. These companies expect work at any hour of the day, but give the employee little recognition or reward for the disruption costs that 24-hour work entails. These curmudgeon companies' notion of additional perks for employee flexibility may consist of picking up the check for pizzas or curry during a late night. Unfortunately, this is a familiar picture in some companies that globalize. They want to be multi-time zone but do not consider the profound change in culture that this requires.

On the other side of the divide, employees can be resistant to delivering their side of the pact too, refusing to make any schedule adjustments. While visiting companies, we have heard countless gripes about individuals who are inflexible. In one British–California collaboration where there was an eight-hour time difference, it was evident that at least one side needed to timeshift somewhat. During one project phase of urgent software fixes, the stubborn British technical expert insisted on starting the day early, while his equally intransigent California counterpart insisted on coming into the office late. Thus, together they made the time difference even more pronounced than the formal eight hours. Neither side would adjust, resulting in no overlap window for synchronous communication. During this period of urgency all communication between the Brit and the American relied on just one e-mail batch per day from each side.

Nevertheless, like Infosys, some companies successfully create a 24-hour culture. Once created, the organization's continued success pivots on whether the spirit is sustainable over many months and many years. There are risks of employee disillusionment and employee burnout. The toll that 24-hour readiness takes on individuals varies among individuals, but it can be high. We return to this last point in chapter 8.

Radical Strategy #2: Simulated Co-location for Overlapping Time Zones

THE ESSENCE OF THE SIMULATED co-location strategy is to erase both distance and time zone differences as much as is managerially and technologically possible. Time zone differences are erased by strict schedule alignment between the distant sites, which may require some timeshifting. Everyone works during the same time window no matter where they are. Meanwhile, distance is erased by simulated co-location based on always-on audio/video and dashboards.

We call this work arrangement Real-Time Simulated Co-location (RTSC). It is at Level 4, the highest level of our TZR framework (introduced in chapter 4). In RTSC, distant sites collaborate naturally throughout the workday, as if co-located. Technology-wise this isn't complex or expensive anymore. All sites need high-quality, always-on video and audio, and awareness technologies such as a shared dashboard of key project data and status. The elements of simulated co-location have been practiced in a variety of industries. In a large global financial firm such as Deutsche Bank, there are video and audio links between its globe-spanning trading rooms. Decades ago such firms installed always-on squawk boxes, for audio, to connect between distant sites across continents.

The next case, the last in the book, describes one global software company that has successfully implemented RTSC, though we cannot use the company's real name.

CASE STUDY
Agile Factori

Agile Factori is an American agile software consulting company with software development centers in several global locations. The company is a leader in agile methods. These are software development methods that feature intensive, focused work and collaboration in a humanistic environment with minimal bureaucratic nonsense. As is typical in the agile community, for instance, we heard a manager proclaim, "…we don't create one-hundred page specifications documents."

Agile Factori is perhaps fanatical about its agile practices. Undoubtedly, the company has a very strong organizational culture. Most noticeable were the radically co-located team rooms, sometimes called "war rooms," where software developers work together, sitting almost elbow to elbow, talking and listening to others' conversations. All around them on the surrounding walls were charts, dashboards, and up-to-date status information. The co-location was part of the company's organizational culture—its religion. As a matter of principle, team members could not work from home, day or evening.

The company practices a fairly selective approach to hiring, choosing clients, and work style. Consistent with its agile philosophy, the company likes to work very closely with its clients, even when they are very far away. It makes a point of stressing this matter to its potential clients. Some like this work mode; others do not. Working this way with the client is part of this story.

In Houston, a large American client, BigOil, signed an IT application development contract with Agile Factori. BigOil knew that it would work closely with Agile Factori and it requested that the Agile Factori offshore development center be in Brazil because BigOil was doing some business in the country and because Brazil is time zone proximate to BigOil. The third location was BigOil's Dallas office. For cost and resource reasons, the fourth location was at one of Agile Factori's partner subcontractors in Argentina.

continued...

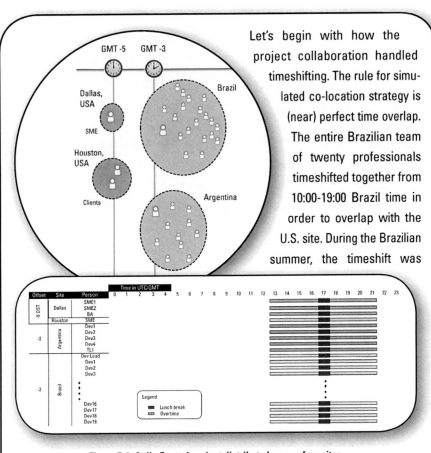

Let's begin with how the project collaboration handled timeshifting. The rule for simulated co-location strategy is (near) perfect time overlap. The entire Brazilian team of twenty professionals timeshifted together from 10:00-19:00 Brazil time in order to overlap with the U.S. site. During the Brazilian summer, the timeshift was

Figure 7-1: Agile Factori project distributed across four sites.
Notice the timeshifting depicted in the line chart with work hour alignment across sites.

more dramatic—12:00 to 21:00. At lunchtime, the South American professionals take a lunch break as a team so that the client can plan around fixed gap times. This norm came about because early in the collaboration, even before mobile numbers had been exchanged, the entire Brazilian team disappeared to have lunch just as the Texas client team was starting its day, causing some consternation.

The most striking thing that one saw in each of the four team rooms was the prominent high-resolution, real-time video screens. Two of the displays showed teams of roughly twenty developers in their offices in Brazil and Argentina. The other two screens showed smaller clusters of BigOil's key people in Texas. Audio

continued...

and video were always on. Microphones sat just below the display. One could walk over to the big screens and hear some of the hustle and bustle at the other locations. More importantly, just by walking over to the screen area, Michael in the Houston location could spontaneously video-meet with Gisele at the Brazilian location.

Awareness was very high between the sites. Awareness is one of those subtle concepts that we introduced in chapter 4. First, there was visual awareness. Sitting in Brazil, one could see when a BigOil collaborator came into the office. Even more significant, if one looked up to the screen they could "sense" from a collaborator's body language whether he or she was about to call them. The Houston client was pleased because whenever she looked up to the screens, she could see the team members in the three locations actively engaged in their work. The client also got to know the outsourced software developers on a friendly basis, even though all of them were far away.

The other facets of awareness came from the extensive work dashboard. The dashboard appeared prominently on one of the screens displayed at every site. It was a color-coded display of all the in-process software components with the three possible status indicators of pass, fail, unstable.[89] Thus, one could get an instant sense of progress. Alongside this was a dashboard display of typical project management data.

Agile Factori's culture is deeply rooted in the agile values of co-located work, so it is important to note how the company chose to adapt these deep values in a distributed setting by creating synchronicity and fostering new norms. They used familiar agile methodology elements for work done between distant sites. "Daily standup meetings" were easily done with time overlap and good video, and similarly for agile "retrospectives." Even the famous "paired programming," which couples two programmers to sit together and collaborate on software coding, is doable across a distance. Specifically, remote pairing was attained with Skype and a shared ID on the Eclipse software development platform. In addition, all project software developers had daily access to the Texas-based Subject Matter Experts (SMEs) and could ask these SMEs questions whenever they wished.

Summary

THE RADICAL TIME ZONE STRATEGIES described in this chapter are categorized as radical for a reason. They are not intended for most organizations. The 24-hour culture is demanding and is not necessary for those companies that encounter occasional time zone challenges. It is appropriate for organizations with sharp East–West or far-flung configurations. The simulated co-location strategy is only useful for configurations having some overlap in their time zones, not for collaboration across hemispheres.

Both radical strategies are premised on a strong organizational culture. Certainly, both firms showcased here were elitist firms with strong cultures that impacted their corporate success. Case in point: people at Agile Factori contend that their culture of real-time simulated co-location makes for happier workers, high job satisfaction, and low turnover. Other companies may be able to create the right culture to support the radical strategies in this chapter. Clearly, creating this culture for a young company tends to be easier as evidenced by the many tiny young virtual companies that have quickly ramped-up to a 24-hour culture.

ACTIONABLE ITEMS

- **24-hour buy-in.** The key to making the 24-hour culture successful is for employees to be part of building it. So, implementation requires discussion throughout the unit.
- **24-hour pampering.** Small perks like free coffee are insufficient to make up for the demands of a 24/7 work environment. Companies need to be truly committed to pampering employees with necessary support, facilities and flexibility to make the 24-hour culture tolerable.
- **Always-on technologies.** Set up always-on video, audio, and text at all sites, even in public areas like hallways and coffee rooms.
- **Don't do it**. Assess strategic objectives first. Neither of the two rather difficult radical strategies is worth doing unless the organization gains a competitive advantage from instituting them.

SECTION III
Time And A Half

TIME AND A HALF is the old expression for the 150% pay rate when working overtime. In that spirit, we include these last chapters.

Chapter 8 is about health and well-being issues related to working across time zones. Given that time zone separation demands timeshifting, sometimes too often, these topics merit consideration: medical and social well-being, the biology of circadian rhythms, and labor regulations.

Chapter 9 examines perceptions of time. After all, humans' time perspectives are highly subjective. Each individual has different time visions and these are influenced by his/her group, gender, culture, and societal rhythms. Time separation introduces periods of quiet, which is why we also take a look at the sub-discipline of interruption science.

Finally, Chapter 10 is more theoretical. As business professors we sometimes quote Kurt Lewin and tell our students: "There is nothing more practical than a good theory." We have written this chapter for non-academic readers who are interested in the underlying foundations of how coordination works.

CHAPTER 8

Are They Getting Any Sleep? Health and Well-being

Are They Getting Any Sleep? Health and Well-being

Remember Frank Li from chapter 3? He was the software engineer and trainer at IBM Chengdu who was regularly scheduled to work the second shift. Why? Because he was collaborating with the Americans and, supposedly, everyone on this collaboration required synchronized work. The trouble for Frank, though, was that the meetings began to intensify late at night, China time, so it was hard to unwind at midnight. Sometimes he and others had to stay quite late.

IVEN THAT TIME ZONE SEPARATION demands timeshifting, sometimes quite often, it is important to know more about the various consequences for companies and individuals. Shiftwork and night work affect workers' medical and social well-being. This chapter examines these implications. We also examine the biology of circadian rhythms and end with some notes about labor regulations.

Timeshifting May be Hazardous to Your Health

MANY YEARS AGO, all American cigarette packs had the following printed warning: *cigarette smoking may be hazardous to your health*. Similar warnings are needed for timeshifting. The phrase *may be hazardous to your health* is appropriate for this new age of timeshifting since the science is still somewhat young. However, research has been conducted for decades on shiftwork and night shift and their impacts. The results of this research point to caution and need for moderation.

The impact of night work

There is overwhelming evidence that working the night shift is bad for one's health.[90] The list of impacts is long and dismal. Studies show that working night shifts on a regular basis increases the risk of heart disease. Night shift is often the cause of poor sleep and chronic fatigue. Those who regularly get less than six or seven hours of sleep per night are straining their bodies and tend to have shorter lives. Women's reproductive health is also affected. Night shift workers are at higher risk for breast and colon cancer, possibly because they lack the hormone melatonin to help curb the growth of tumor cells. It is exposure to light during the night shift that reduces melatonin levels. Melatonin also serves as an antioxidant and memory aide. Night shift workers also have high levels of insulin resistance, which is basically lowered sensitivity in the muscle, liver and fat cells to the actions of insulin. Insulin is a hormone that helps convert sugars from food into energy. This outcome is similar to results in sleep studies—lack of sleep seems to disrupt the body's ability to use insulin. Insulin resistance puts people at increased risk for Type 2 diabetes. Other physical problems include ten times normal risk of ulcers.

Additionally, the irregular hours leads to all kinds of mental health risks including stress, depression, and fatigue. There are performance related problems due to slower reaction times. Night workers tend to cut corners and have less empathy.

Not surprisingly, night shift workers are more likely to be involved in accidents. There is a 50% increase in the risk of a vehicle crash for workers driving at 03:00 after four successive night shifts, and even higher at the end of a shift at 07:00. The famous catastrophic industrial accidents of recent decades were all during night shifts: Three Mile Island (1979, United States, nuclear), Bhopal (1984, India, chemical) and Chernobyl (1986, USSR, nuclear).

Adjusting in and out of night shift work is slow and similar to jet lag in that it affects one's circadian system. Although travelers adapt to the new time zone, shift workers usually live out of phase with the local time zone. On top of all of the above, there is a *social toll* to shift working. It shows up in increased divorce rates and higher rates of substance abuse, depression, and stress on the job. Social relationships are also affected since most social activities take place during the daytime hours.

The only consolation for timeshifters is that there is one time zone where it is worse. Travel to outer space is actually the most extreme shiftworking environment and the result is that space crews sleep poorly.

Stress from overtime and from the e-mail deluge

Time zone separation usually requires overtime work because of timeshifting and also because of the need for more detailed explanations and clarifications. It is rare in our studies of tech companies to find a company for which employees worked only forty hours per week. In the

United States, overtime in the tech sector has always been common. U.S. government data shows that about 500,000 American computer professionals work fifty or more hours per week.[91] It is now more common in Europe than it once was (in 2005, *Businessweek* reported a 10% jump in Germans working overtime[92]). Overtime is very common in the new tech nations like China and India. Excessive overtime, similar to working the night shift, has health implications. For example, the classic Whitehall studies, a large-scale analysis of British civil servants, found that consistent work of fifty-five hours or more has a higher risk of sleep problems.[93]

Whether or not they work excessive overtime, global knowledge workers feel pressured. First, they are time pressured. "Faster is better" is the mantra that drives business. For this reason, they are even rushed at mealtime (one-third of American workers eat lunch at their desks[94]). Second, they feel pressured to check and respond to messages. Many addictively check their messages or other mobile device (recall the time when BlackBerry phones were called "Crackberry" because they were as addicting as crack cocaine). These pressures and addictions can create stress.

The stress on workers is also due to the batched work that arrives overnight from time zones to the east. Barley and colleagues[95] studied dozens of tech workers and found that while there were fewer interruptions when working with colleagues many time zones away, there was a sense of relentless overload. The workers came into work in the morning with a batch of backlogged messages that "exacerbate[d] people's sense of being overloaded." This accumulates all day, building up anxieties about falling further behind because, after all, the expectations and norms are of immediate response.

Taking Control and the Work–life Balance

SCATTERTIME, introduced in chapter 1, interacts closely with work-life balance. Balance is not necessarily understood to mean that available time is split equally between work and home, but rather that individuals have different expectations and preferences for the ways they organize their schedules. Each generation has different notions about the desirable mix of work and non-work life. Leisure time is not a term our great-grandparents would have understood, what with all the household chores that were a part of their life (food preparation, for instance, required much more time then).

Dale Southernton[96] uses the term *hot spots* and *cold spots* to describe scheduling of work, household chores, and leisure. True leisure is squeezed between blocks of time constrained by other scheduled commitments like work, sleep, and chores. These are the scheduled "hotspots." Whatever is left are the "cold spots," the unscheduled time around which family and friends can enjoy themselves.

Stress can be reduced and healthier choices can be made if individuals perceive work factors being under their control, or if empowered to design their jobs and their schedules. The well-known *Karasek-Theorell job strain model* has two main components of stress: high job demands (the need to work quickly and hard) and low decision latitude (employees are given the ability to make decisions related to the way they work, including time allocation). Research such as the classic Whitehall civil servants study shows that job strain and poor health came from low decision latitude.[97]

Measuring work-life balance is tricky. It is clearly subjective, but it can be measured somewhat at the national level. One place to begin is for each country to tabulate the annual time off from work. The objective comparison number should be an annual statutory minimum number of vacation days plus public holidays. Presumably more time off is better, except, of course, for workaholics. We have found these national counts vary quite a bit from one source to the next. So with that qualifier in mind, here are representative data from the well-regarded Mercer 2009[98] study: "Employees in Brazil and Lithuania would have the world's most generous holiday regime with a potential forty-one days off a year, while those in Finland, France and Russia could receive a total of forty days. In contrast, Canadian employees receive only nineteen days, Chinese employees twenty-one, and those in the United States and Singapore twenty-five."

We mentioned the different workweeks earlier in this book. For example, the official Dutch workweek is thirty-nine hours and the Japanese is forty-two hours. A simple calculation interprets the remaining hours in the week as leisure hours. But commute time and chores are probably not leisure. How could leisure time be measured anyway? Some cultures tend to sleep more. The French are found to sleep the most of all Europeans—over nine hours per night on average. *Peut-être* they best maximize leisure?

Circadian Rhythms

NEARLY ALL LIFE, from plants, bacteria and insects (including cockroaches), jellyfish, all the way to humans, live on 24-hour cycles.[99] All living things are exposed to the daily change in natural light intensity that allows them to organize their rest activities according to 24-hour cycles.[100] Thus, all organisms have a *circadian rhythm* that allows synchronization with the light and dark cycles created by the Earth's rotation. One daily rhythm is a person's body temperature, which gets cues from the natural light (see fig. 8-1).

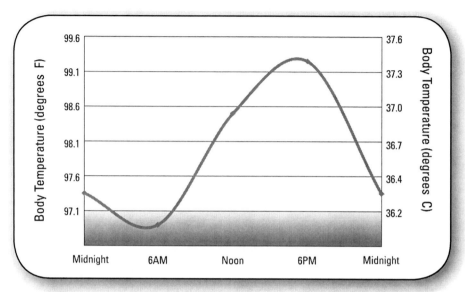

Figure 8-1: Average human body temperature indicating circadian rhythm during a 24-hour period.[101]

Researchers who study the temporal dimension of life and its daily rhythms are called chronobiologists. Worldwide, there are over one thousand chronobiologists/scientists working on the basic science of biological time.[102] The science can help us understand what time is best for work. The best time in the day for doing a job *varies by task!* For example, complex problem solving or logical reasoning is best done around noon. Tasks that rely on physical coordination, like sports, are best performed in the early evening when the body temperature is at its peak.[103]

The science also gives a picture of how flexible one can be within the all-powerful rhythm. Human volunteers have gone deep underground and stayed in constant light environment for weeks on end in order to help chronobiologists learn more about the circadian rhythm. With no way of knowing the day from the night, the body rhythms begin to drift away from the rhythm of the outside world… and then it drifts back. The body can be trained for different daily rhythms. In fact, all organisms can be pushed a little bit outside the circadian rhythm by 24 +/- 2 hours, but not much more.[104]

It would be profitable for global workers to rid themselves of the need for sleep. The body can be pushed in that direction for short periods with drugs, such as modafinil. Modafinil, a so-called eugeroic, is an effective stimulant. It is the drug of choice for militaries such as those in the United States or the French Foreign Legion to keep the soldiers fighting. It is available with prescription in the United States. But it is not recommended for everyday timeshifters.

In the future, probably well before the next century, humans will need less sleep. It is quite conceivable that bioengineers will produce individuals, through genetic engineering, who don't require sleep. The military R&D, especially the American and the British, has been very interested in prolonging the workday of the soldier. The U.S. military is said to have spent $100 million on research to help soldiers called "metabolically dominant soldiers," sleep less or not at all.

Another form of shiftwork that throws off the body's circadian rhythm is jet lag. It is disruptive and affects one's health and well-being. Studies of jetlagged laboratory mice and flight attendants point to similar conclusions. One study scanned the brains of female flight attendants who had been flying across time zones for many years and found evidence of impaired thinking ability.[105] According to another study, elderly mice die earlier if they are exposed to timeshifting that replicates the effects of jet lag.

The jet lag rule of thumb is that it takes about one day to adjust for each time zone crossed, though the different organs in one's body have different adjustment periods.[106] The liver may be the slowest, taking up to two weeks to catch up. The direction one flies makes a difference. There is evidence that indicates traveling east is more difficult for most people and therefore takes them slightly longer to adjust. One study that confirmed the east-is-worse finding followed U.S. Army soldiers transferring from the United States to Europe and vice versa.[107] This east-versus-west question is similar to traditional shiftwork in which forward rotation shiftwork (described in chapter 3) is easier for humans to handle than backwards rotation shifts.[108]

Labor Laws Regarding Night Work and Overtime

NIGHT WORK is considered so egregious that in 1990 the International Labor Organization (ILO) passed a special set of guidelines that apply to anything that directly touches the span from 00:00 to 05:00.[109] The ILO sets forth the rights of employees to undergo a health assessment, and the right of a worker to transfer to a different shift if night shifts impact the person's health.

Interestingly, there are very few nations that ratified this treaty. The United States, India, most nations in the European Union, and most other high-tech nations have not ratified it.

A sample regulation is: "Night workers must enjoy a level of health and safety protection commensurate with the nature of their work. Protection and prevention facilities must be equivalent to those of other workers and must be available at all times." European Directive 2003/88/EC, the Working Time Directive, is similar in thrust, though less confining. It, too, has not been fully implemented in many of the member states.

In contrast to night work, *overtime work* tends to be more tightly regulated all over the world. Governments tend to place some protections when working long and unsociable hours. In the workweek norm, there is the standard workweek, the overtime in-between period, and a no-fly zone of excessive hours per week. The standard regulated workweek ranges from thirty-seven hours in Denmark, forty hours in the United States, forty-three hours in Israel, forty-four in Brazil, and up to fifty hours in India. But in global firms, the international norm is forty hours, unless it is shortened by national regulation.

The EU does not permit more than forty-eight hours per week, including any overtime. In the UK, Working Time Regulations were passed as a result of EU Directive 93/104/EC. Thus, UK employers are now required to take all reasonable steps to ensure that workers do not work more than an average of forty-eight hours a week over a seventeen week period. Rest periods are also mandated. Workers must have a rest period of at least eleven consecutive hours in each 24-hour period and an uninterrupted rest period of at least twenty-four hours in each seven-day period.

ACTIONABLE ITEMS

- **Beware night shift.** Night shift needs management attention in ways that other shifts do not: health and behavioral problems are inevitable. So, mitigate these with food, flexibility, and any incentives that reduce stress. In the coming years, unions and governments all over the world are likely to target this issue.
- **Build up time zone resistance.** Individuals can improve hardiness in time zone/ timeshifting/jetlag through better awareness.

CHAPTER 9

Perceptions of Time

Perceptions of Time

The far-flung work team spanned five time zones and as many cultures. The weekly ninety-minute conference call was a vital coordination mechanism. Here are two contrasting composite narratives of these conference calls.

Manager #1, from a concrete time culture, relates: "The members from my time culture feel that everyone's attention needs to focus on the task during those precious ninety-minute weekly conference calls and we are exasperated when colleagues from the elastic time culture not only show up late but also need five minutes of small talk whenever they join. Then they even take interruptions during the conference call that seem to be non-emergency calls."

Manager #2, from an elastic time culture, says: "Most of us on this team have never met face-to-face; and we've done just one videoconference at the kick-off, and then it became "too much of a problem." So, team members from my time culture anticipate that when we deal with our counterparts at the other sites we need to build long-term trusting relationships. But my counterparts from the concrete time culture plunge straight into a discussion of some small detail and I don't really know the person, I cannot tell if I can trust him."

MUCH OF THE FIRST eight chapters implicitly assume that time and time zones are objective entities. But humans' time perspectives are, without question, highly subjective. As these narratives[110] hint, each individual has different time visions and, these are influenced by his or her group, gender, culture, and broad societal rhythms. The debate about whether time separation is good or bad is also informed by the individuals' ability to handle interruptions. We begin with the topic of rhythm.

The Societal Rhythms of Time

HAVEN'T YOU NOTICED that when you look at a snapshot, whether it is taken in an office, at home, or at a gathering, you can intuitively tell what time of day the photo was taken? That's because the photo conveys hints of deeply ingrained daily rhythms that are second nature to all of us—it is the societal rhythms of time.

Sociologist Eviatar Zerubavel[111] spent his career studying the sociology of time and writes extensively about the internal rhythm of time, summarized briefly here. One of the dimensions of rhythm is the *schedule*: that innocuous artifact that is the rhythm we all live by, like a metronome in our lives. Academics call this *temporal regularity:* the phenomenon that involves the structuring of social life by forcing activities into fairly rigid temporal patterns.

The schedule is one of the institutions most characteristic of Western civilization and originally evolved in the medieval Benedictine monasteries of Europe. In the monastery, monks constructed the table of hours, the *horarium*, meaning the schedule. The rhythm was created by the reading of the full cycle of one hundred fifty Psalms, which began each Sunday. From that horarium, various novel elements brought about regularity to their lives, to the larger community, and eventually to all communities all over Christian Europe. One example of how the horarium worked is that, to mark the periods of the day and the time of religious services, the monks rang the monastery bells.

Food was another dimension that helped shape the monastery's horarium. The rotation of kitchen service was balanced with prayer and work: "The brethren then shall rise at the eighth hour of the night so that their sleep might extend for a moderate space beyond midnight." Mealtime, especially lunchtime, became regular. The monks ate when it was lunchtime, not necessarily when they were hungry. Around this period, some of the monasteries began to have access to an important new invention, the mechanical clock. The clock helped to reinforce the schedule.

The Benedictine order bequeathed its utilitarian philosophy of time to Western civilization at large,[112] causing the literary shift in the 14th century when important writers began publishing discourses with titles that conveyed a sense of the importance of time and timeliness:

Of Leisure and the Loss of Time

What Reasons Lead Us to Conserve and Keep an Account of Time?

How Great a Vice It Is to Delay Doing Good Works

These are titles that would hardly be noticeable today, but back then conveyed attitudes about time that created new societal norms.

Today the world views a lack of time rhythm as being remarkable. In 2011, anthropologists studying remote tribes in the Amazon came to an astonishing finding captured in this BBC headline:[113] "An Amazonian tribe has no abstract concept of time, say researchers. The Amondawa lacks the linguistic structures that relate time and space—as in our idea of, for example, 'working through the night.'"

In this next part of the chapter, we move from society to the individual.

Psychological Clocks: Individual Perceptions of Time

" *Time flies when you're having fun.* **"**
Common adage

THE GREATER THE URGENCY, the slower time passes. Anyone who has waited for a kettle of water to boil, or waited for a bus, is well aware of this. Cognitive psychologists have studied these common folklores about time and confirmed that each individual has a subjective perception of time, and that those perceptions are likely to vary depending on the situation. By time perception we mean that different people have different perceptions of certain objective units of time such as seconds or days. Studies have found that age is a factor in time perception. Both young children and older adults are less accurate in assessing time. Gender is also a factor. Females tend to underestimate the duration of a short interval of time, while males tend to overestimate it.[114] Also, not surprisingly, practice and training improve our judgment of time.

Given that the pace of life and work keeps getting faster and faster, Blatchley and colleagues[115] conducted a study to see if the ubiquitous computer has affected time perception. Subjects had to judge the duration of a series of time intervals ranging from three to twenty-seven seconds. Participants who were the heaviest computer users tended to be the most accurate in estimating the passage of time.

In addition to the circadian rhythms described in the previous chapter, individuals have personal tendencies for morning or evening, referred to as "larks" and "owls," respectively. That is, larks are morning people who are the most alert early and prefer demanding mental tasks early. Owls are evening people who are most alert in the late evening hours, do demanding work later, and go to bed later.[116] Most people fall in between. When the rhythm of larks or owls is disrupted, very much like jet lag, performance is disrupted.

Group Rhythms and Deadlines

The first mechanical clocks began appearing about 1300 A.D.
" *and since then we have been steadily losing the battle with time.* **"** [117]

AT THE BEGINNING OF A PROJECT, when its members are forged and socialized together into a project team, the team begins to establish its team time rhythm and its own special sense of milestones and deadlines. This team rhythm doesn't evolve in a vacuum, though. It is very much influenced at the onset from rhythms that come from the outside. The environment outside the team tends to set much of the pace. The organizational rules, the corporate culture, monthly meetings, quarterly reports, the fiscal year, the industry norms, and the general economy all play a part.

For a new team to work together well, it is essential to sync the individual members' different time perceptions. This is vital if the external rhythms are somewhat blurry, something that may happen if the organizational time culture is not strong, or if the team was formed from individuals from several companies.

Establishing a team rhythm is best achieved by discussing and agreeing to the key team time norms upfront: punctuality, promptness in responding to messages, revolving schedules, escalation of urgency, and seriousness of deadlines. Naturally, not all teams form effective team rhythms; some teams stay in dissonance forever. Thankfully, most teams develop a rhythm. Even so, these rhythms are fragile and can be "punctured," usually when a crisis happens. A puncture disrupts everybody's sense of time and is somewhat analogous to group jetlag.[118]

The group's rhythm is also influenced by whether or not it embraces "time management." Time management tools like list-making, prioritization, group calendars, scheduling, and others are quite familiar. So, presumably, time management training, which improves skills with such tools, produces positive results. As it turns out, however, a research review by Claessens and colleagues[119] concludes that time management training does not seem to lead to better performance, though this does not mean the performance gets worse. Where time management training does make a difference is in the individuals' perceived control of time and job satisfaction, leading to better health and reduced stress. Perhaps this result is well worth the investment in time management training.

Cultural Differences and Time

NOT ONLY DO INDIVIDUALS have different notions of time, but perceptions of time and tempo vary by culture as well. It is well accepted that different cultures treat all matters of time quite differently, even though time itself is an absolute.[120]

Since those who are globally connected are obsessed with speed, let's begin with the culture of speed. Robert Levine conducted a fascinating cross-cultural comparison of speed. He refers to speed as tempo, and studied it in different cities around the world by carefully observing and measuring three key behaviors: how fast people walk along the sidewalk, the accuracy of city clocks, and the working speed of postal clerks. He compiled and ranked the cities from fastest to slowest in tempo. Which global locations have the fastest pace of life?[121] Answer: The fastest pace of life is in a city we associate with clocks—Zürich. It is followed by Dublin, Frankfurt, Tokyo and then Rome. The only American city listed, New York City, is ranked sixteenth.

At one end of the cultural continuum are those cultures that see time as *concrete*. In a concrete time culture, deadlines are firm and strict. People are punctual to meetings. Time is objective in these cultures. Time is seen as made up of small units that are all alike; a minute is a minute! Time is a scarce resource; it is precious. Germans and Americans tend to view time as concrete.

At the other end are those cultures that tend to see time as *elastic*. Deadlines are flexible. Meeting times are soft targets and arriving at the meeting twenty minutes after the scheduled time is acceptable. Cultures that tend to be time elastic include Latinos, Indians, Arabs, and to some extent, the French. Peruvian social time, for example, means that if you are invited to a party at 20:00, you don't show up until at least 21:00, or even later, or else it would be considered impolite because the hosts would not be ready.

These contradictory cultural time differences lead to perceptions of "the other." The concrete time culture tends to see the elastic time culture as slow and inefficient; being late is equated with rudeness and disrespect and can have a damaging effect on relationships, reliability, and credibility. In contrast, the elastic time culture tends to see the concrete time culture as cold and rigid.[122] Edward Hall, in his seminal 1959 book on attributes of cultures, introduced these classic time-culture constructs as monochronic (which we call concrete) and polychronic (which we call elastic).[123]

Interestingly, multitasking has different motivations in the elastic and concrete time cultures. In concrete time cultures multitasking appears when people are trying to get through their endless To Do lists; thus they end up doing many things simultaneously in order to "save" time and be more efficient. But multitasking in elastic time cultures does not stem from efficiency. Rather, it is the result of a strong sense of duty or loyalty to others who have requested something, perhaps a favor. This demonstrates the stronger focus on relationships that is typical of elastic time cultures.

Different cultural perceptions of time are not defined simply by national boundaries. Within the United States, for example, minority groups make a point of distinguishing their time from that of the white hegemonic time, which is seen as a concrete clock culture. The Native Americans talk about "living on Indian time," African-Americans formerly used the term "colored people's time,"[124] and Jewish Americans use the term "Jewish standard time."

In this next and last part of this chapter, we move from the subjective perceptions of time to the cognitive perceptions of time.

Cognitive Issues:
Interruptions Versus Quiet Time

WE CONTEND THAT AS GADGETS get ever more invasive, *quiet time* will become more valuable. Quiet time is the time to focus on imaginative, complex work, without interruptions.[125] Separating a project team across many time zones may cause delays and miscommunication, but it does have at least one silver lining—it likely reduces the number of interruptions during the traditional workday. Fewer phone calls, e-mails, tweets, and chat messages are coming in while the individual is trying to think. Researchers are now positing that frequent distractions lead to cognitive overload, which leads to tension with colleagues and in personal relationships, which in turn leads to a decline in job satisfaction.

Certainly there is some contrariety on this topic. In much of this book we emphasize the need to create and manage timeshifting—striving for connectivity and very tight synchronicity. Synchronicity implies many interruptions. Nevertheless, here we introduce a drawback with this approach.

Quiet Time

We've noticed that those tech workers who work in time zone-separated configurations crave the quiet time that it affords. For example, Frank of IBM Chengdu often worked second shift—

from 15:00 to 24:00—in order to overlap with his project partners far away. His cherished quiet time occurred in his early afternoon before the Americans came to work; he used this time to concentrate on moving his tasks forward before the daily interruptions began.

Knowledge workers use quiet time to do higher-order cognitive tasks that seem impossible in a busy office where messages, meetings, and distractions are common interrupters of the workday. As a result, individuals have their favorite spots or times of day to grab some quiet time to engage in quiet concentration. Researchers speculate that workers need such quiet time to tackle creative tasks and this time is also an essential part of learning and creativity. Interestingly, Gloria Mark and her colleagues[126] found that afternoon tasks were longer in duration, probably because workers delayed cognitively complex tasks until the afternoon when perhaps they had fewer interruptions. This is worth pondering, particularly when thinking about schedules across time zones.

Distractions

Researchers have documented the enormity of distractions. The knowledge worker sitting in front of her computer is distracted thirty seven times per hour.[127] Mark and colleagues also found that 57% of an individual's tasks are interrupted,[128] and co-located people work longer before switching tasks but have more interruptions.

All of this knowledge about how people focus on tasks calls for a new specialty discipline that perhaps wasn't needed just a few years ago. The pundits have named this discipline *distraction science*. Other names include interruption science, the study of multitasking, information overload,[129] distraction overload, and continuous partial attention.

In 2007 Basex,[130] a research consultancy came up with a stunning statistic: $588 billion a year is lost in productivity due to work time interruptions in the U.S. economy. While we think these extrapolations made by Basex are overstated, they do give one pause to stop and think about the potential impact work time interruptions have on work.

Yet, there are those who argue that distractions are not so bad. One has probably heard the assertion that young knowledge workers have become better at *multitasking* because of all the computer games and gadgets that digital natives have. False. The human brain is fast, but unlike even an ancient computer operating system, the brain is not well programmed for rapid and efficient task switching. Humans have trouble switching between tasks. In fact, they cannot seem do more than one thing at a time, at least not very well. This could be because upon exiting a task one must store that task's state, and upon entering the next task context (another environment) one must retrieve its task state.

Regardless of whether a worker believes that distractions are overwhelming or relishes multitasking, there are knowledge workers who are addicted to the distraction of messages, much like those with drug addictions. The conditioning to react and inspect a message gives the reader a small shot of the brain's chemical dopamine, which brings pleasure.[131]

So, where was I? More on the field of distraction science appears in a rather entertaining interview in Appendix D, titled "So Where Was I?" This is a conversation on workplace interruptions with Gloria Mark of the University of California at Irvine. The interview originally appeared in *Information Overload Forum* in 2008 and appears verbatim in this book with permission.

Contrary Studies

The study of overload and distractions is still relatively young so, naturally, there are contrary studies. For example, researchers have studied software engineers for decades now, and some have found that they actually adjust to distractions and perform at higher levels when in a more high-intensity environment such as "extreme programming" in which developers work in pairs. Gumm[132] asserts that too much is made of the advantage of undisturbed work. The advantage of isolation and smaller teams is not in reduced interruptions as she claims from her study, but in the advantage of better team autonomy, esprit de corps, cohesion, and motivation. In fact, she argues that, from the project perspective, co-location puts more pressure on the timeline because of the danger that the tardy programmer will be seen in the hall or at lunch and will lose face by having to explain herself. Separately, Teasley and colleagues[133] studied "radical co-location," which is the very tight seating arrangement that we now commonly see in agile team-rooms. These tight seating arrangements are not conceived to save on office space. Rather, they are meant to accelerate sharing of knowledge. The researchers found that software engineers quickly get used to this distraction-laden environment.

There are those who argue that some cultures are better able to cope with distractions and interruptions. Certainly the open-space seating in much of the world (and at some American firms such as HP) suggests cultural influence. For example, at Brazilian technology firms, office architecture is often spaced very tightly together and is susceptible to distractions.

Final Note

WHAT DO THESE VARIED TIME PERCEPTIONS mean for collaborators dispersed across time zones? The material in this chapter should make evident that any impact will vary from one individual to the next. One particular timeshifting approach may work fine for one team but may be a stomach-churning experience for another team with different time perceptions.

ACTIONABLE ITEMS

- **Team rhythm.** Discuss and agree on the key team time norms up front namely, revolving schedules, punctuality, promptness in responding to messages, escalation of urgency, and seriousness of deadlines.
- **Know your teammate's time perceptions.** Educate yourself and your team about perceptions of time across cultures and organizations. Is your counterpart a concrete time person or an elastic time person? You need to know this.
- **Quiet.** Maximize quiet time systematically. Set aside no-meeting slots during non-overlap times.

CHAPTER 10

Theoretical Perspectives on Coordination Challenges

Theoretical Perspectives on Coordination Challenges

I F YOU HAVE READ THIS FAR you are most definitely interested in learning how to work effectively across time zones. In this chapter we put it all together, but from a theoretical perspective. We believe the theory will help you better understand some of the challenges and solutions for time zone separation. The Time Zone Framework diagrammed in figure 10-1 encapsulates the theoretical understanding of the topic. It is also the guide to this entire chapter.

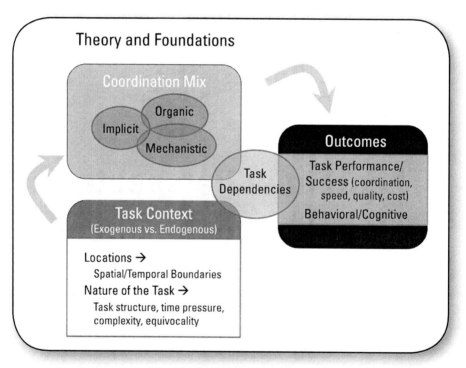

Figure 10-1: The Time Zone Framework.

Let's walk along the logic of the framework. We begin at the top left with the *Coordination Mix* of tactics employed by team members and managers to coordinate the task work (i.e., to manage its dependencies). Clockwise, the next is *Outcomes*, which are the end results that organizations care about. These are the performance outcomes of success and failure. But, there are also non-task outcomes to keep in mind—coordination and behavioral/cognitive. Last, as we travel clockwise back to the beginning, is the *Task Context.*

However, before these components are presented in more detail, we briefly go back to the middle, the heart of the diagram—*Task Dependencies.* You've read about task dependencies in several places in this book. Dependencies represent the extent to which team members need each other in order to get the work done. When there are zero dependencies, there are no coordination issues and time zone separation becomes irrelevant because team members work independently. In contrast, when there are high dependencies, collaborators constantly check each other's work and cannot move on until the other has finished. Most dependencies fall somewhere in between those extreme points. To illustrate this we go back to the kitchen examples: Three chefs preparing a feast can divide the preparation into salads, entrees, and pastry; once the menu has been coordinated they can then work quite independently.

Coordination Mix: Mechanistic, Organic, and Implicit

THE KEY SOLUTIONS to time zone separation were introduced in chapters 3 and 4: timeshifting, sync solutions, and async solutions. Now let's turn to theory to get a deeper understanding of these solutions. Through a theoretical lens, project teams have a palette of three types of coordination tactics they can use to mitigate the problems of time zones—mechanistic, organic and implicit. They are defined as follows:

Mechanistic coordination involves processes or practices used to manage predictable and routine dependencies in a task. These are structured into things you recognize, such as project schedules, plans, specifications, roles, division of labor, and workflow tools.[134]

Organic coordination involves processes or practices based on communication and interaction, which are necessary for the less-predictable and less-certain aspects of the task. This coordination appears in things you recognize from work such as team meetings, one-on-one voice conversations, debriefings, e-mails, announcements, and memos. Nobel Prize winner management theorist Herbert Simon was one of the early thinkers on this aspect of coordination.[135]

Implicit coordination is based on unspoken assumptions about what others are likely to do.[136] This coordination derives from knowledge about things around you like knowing whether the collaborator is available at her desk or about to take a coffee break; or knowing what she's working on now and next; or, whether she knows the answer to your question or can point you to the right person who knows the answer. Thus, implicit coordination is achieved from knowledge that collaborators have about each other and about the task activities of others on the team.

More on implicit coordination

Implicit coordination warrants further discussion because it is subtle, yet so important. All implicit coordination mechanisms are based on knowledge that team members have about each other, their tasks, and their surroundings. This knowledge about other team members— who they are, which expertise they possess, and what work they do—helps develop accurate expectations about what is needed for the task and how to work with others. Knowledge about the surroundings is better known as "situation awareness,"[137] which has been studied extensively in the military for pilots as well as foot soldiers.

Because implicit coordination helps individuals anticipate what others will do, it helps teams coordinate with less (organic) communication. This is a great asset when working across time zones. Not only that, but the team's *shared knowledge* about their work also makes organic and mechanistic coordination more effective because team members have more accurate mental representations of things that they deal with such as procedures and vocabulary. The downside is that when the team is dispersed, implicit coordination is difficult to catalyze because the shared knowledge, the history, isn't there. That shared knowledge can become deeper after face-to-face meetings, when individuals get to know each other.

Team knowledge also has *durability*. This knowledge can be durable or fleeting.[138] Durability doesn't mean how long members can retain the knowledge, but rather how long the knowledge is relevant to the task. Knowledge about one's task areas and of others in the team (e.g., a test engineer's knowledge about software design) and the knowledge about other team members' expertise (i.e., knowing who is an expert at what) are examples of durable knowledge because they are relevant over the long term. Knowledge about who did what recently (e.g., whether developers have finished coding the software) or knowledge about who is around when needed (i.e., presence awareness) are two examples of fleeting knowledge because they are only relevant during specific situations.

The mixer

Team members adopt a *portfolio* of mechanistic, organic and implicit coordination tactics when collaborating on a task. The key to successful coordination is adopting an optimal *coordination mix* of coordination tactics, and then performing them well. As with many managerial recipes, there is no one correct mix. Two divergent coordination tactic portfolios may both be equally effective in helping teams coordinate. For instance, one team may resort to intensive communications (i.e., organic) whereas another may rely on rigorous procedures and division of labor (i.e., mechanistic). Nonetheless, the wisdom on the coordination mix is that mechanistic is good for routine work, organic is good for non-routine work, and implicit is good for real-time, fast-paced tasks.

But now, we come back to the middle of the framework—the dependencies. An effective mechanistic coordination method is to subdivide the task into groups of activities that are relatively independent, like the example of the three chefs given earlier, so that coordination requirements are reduced between groups. This is one rationale for the familiar division of labor. However, such division of labor doesn't work well for some of the tasks that are not *routine*. Organic coordination is preferred, or needed, in such cases. In essence, organic coordination is about communication in many forms: oral, written, interpersonal, in groups, formal and informal. For example, software teams usually have regular formal debriefing meetings, but Kraut and colleagues already noticed years ago that a substantial amount of coordination takes place through spontaneous encounters in public places like hallways, water coolers, and cafeterias.[139]

Some tactics may be more effective for less routine task activities. Organic communication with intensive frequent communication, for instance, is more effective for the case of software development with uncertain and changing requirements. This explains the popularity of practices like extreme programming and agile development.

However, temporal separation severely impairs communication as we've noted repeatedly in this book. So, what does theory say is the best portfolio of coordination for uncertain software activities, in a large-scale collaboration, carried out over multiple time zones? Our collective research suggests that it is some qualified balance between the three coordination types. That is, rigorous mechanistic coordination in concert with strong implicit coordination, augmented when needed by organic coordination during overlapping windows to help the team converge.

In sum, the traditional views of coordination need to be revisited with time zone dispersion. Mechanistic and implicit coordination become more important in temporal-separated environments. These types of coordination need more focused attention, not only to make up for the diminished communication, but also to make this limited communication more effective.

Time zones and synchronicity

The coordination mix is based on long-established research that is applicable to all kinds of teams. But working across time zones changes the coordination needs in yet another way because the smaller time overlap affects the synchronicity of interaction among team members. Alan Dennis and colleagues have been studying communication over distance for decades and have formulated a Media Synchronicity Theory[140] (MST). MST deepens the understanding of organic coordination across time zones because it speaks of how various pipelines, the *media*, support sync or async interaction. According to MST, all communication is composed of a pair of complementary processes—*conveyance* of information and *convergence* on meaning. Conveyance is the transmitting of information. In any collaboration there is a great need for passing information around. The media of choice for that is often e-mail.

The other part of the pair, convergence, led to the term we use throughout the book: *convergence window*. Convergence involves the discussion, processing and interpretation of the information conveyed. Therefore, synchronous interaction, like that via videoconference or telephone, is most effective for the overall success of that type of communication. The objective is to agree on the meaning of the information, which requires individuals to reach a common understanding.

The key insight from MST is that organic coordination is no longer viewed as universally effective for all types of non-routine task activities. Given that time zones create communication challenges, MST's insight is that this is not a problem at all when conveying information. In fact, MST implies that asynchronous interaction like e-mail is most effective for conveyance, and thereby results in better overall communication performance.

Naturally, coordination is only important if it affects outcomes, which we discuss next.

Outcomes

Heard in a tech team conversation: ... **"** *the advantage of distributed work is that you can blame distributed work for the project being late.* **"** [141]

THIS PIECE OF WRY HUMOR brings us to the end point in the framework, which represents the ultimate goal for work teams—outcomes. That is, the degree of success or failure in overcoming time zones when delivering work outputs. Time zones matter if they affect some outcome positively or negatively. The premise is that time zone differences make coordinating work harder. That's why we wrote this book. So let's examine the three outcomes in figure 10-1, performance, coordination, and behavioral/cognitive.

Performance Outcomes. These are most important to management and are quite familiar. For example these outcomes could be the typical triad of any project: on-time delivery (meet schedules), quality (meet requirements, free of errors) and, on budget (no cost overruns).

Coordination Outcomes. These outcomes are best explained in the negative. That is, the extent to which there were no coordination problems during the collaboration, such as integration problems, unsynchronized work schedules, or unresolved process conflicts. All of these tend to be more understated, because managers usually care about coordination outcomes[142] only if they affect performance outcomes. Note that coordination can be costly in that any coordination activity can divert attention from the focal task. It is important, then, to understand when coordination is truly necessary. One team may be effectively coordinated but at an extraordinary cost, thereby driving team performance outcomes down.

Behavioral and Cognitive Outcomes. A project may meet all objective performance indicators, but still have (negative) consequences on team members. In chapter 8, we mentioned some of these. They are fatigue, stress, burnout of timeshifting, and overtime. These outcomes are sometimes ignored because they don't have immediate visible consequences on the project at hand. But in the long run, they may impact the organization's ability to carry out projects effectively across time zones. Behavioral outcomes are those that involve members' actions (e.g., turnover, absenteeism, confrontation), whereas cognitive outcomes are those that affect mental shifts on members. This type of outcome is not visible (e.g., depression, lack of commitment).

Task Context

WORK HAPPENS IN A CONTEXT—the task context. This context includes how team members are arranged across time and space and what type of task they are charged with. The task context influences the coordination mix adopted.

Spatial and temporal boundaries between members

LET'S START WITH SPATIAL SEPARATION. In a co-located task context, the office—the physical distance between individuals—impacts spontaneous communication. Most readers will have discovered from experience that, for example, you rarely see or chat with your co-worker Pedro, who has an office just one floor above you because he is "so far away."

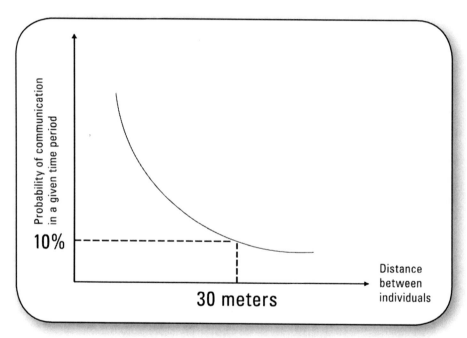

Figure 10-2: The Allen curve showing the probability of spontaneous communication between co-workers.[143]

Tom Allen, in a seminal study from the 1970s, was the first to confirm this when he measured workers' chance encounters and found that spontaneous encounters for people whose offices were more than thirty meters apart were reduced to a chance of only 10% per day (fig. 10-2).

One would think that with today's technologies this curve is a lot flatter,[144] but more recent studies have confirmed that similar curves to the one shown in the Allen curve still apply today.

So, when does a spatial boundary exist in a dyad of two individuals? Is it when the two collaborators are in different offices, hallways, buildings, cities, countries or continents? This question has been an object of fascination ever since the Allen study. McKinsey consultants Siebdrat and colleagues (in fig. 1-2) found performance degradation when the dyad distance is greater than being in the same city. In our own study with Cummings and colleagues[145] we found similar results. A spatial boundary exists when team members are in different cities. It seems that while teams can easily plan co-located meetings when all members reside in the same city, when individuals are located in different cities there is a need for deliberate planning and travel so that the members can meet face to face. This leads to increased coordination costs.

How about temporal boundaries? Our same study showed that a temporal boundary exists in a dyad when there is no work hour overlap for synchronous interaction to help the convergence process, requiring tactics like timeshifting and overtime to meet, and this also leads to increased coordination costs.

Perhaps the difference between spatial and temporal separation seems obvious. We have found that knowledge workers easily confuse, and confound, the effects of temporal and spatial separation. We learned this when we asked participants to describe how they cope with distance or with time zones. We asked them: "What are the main challenges you have experienced when working with others across distance?" We usually got answers like: "We can never find each other because we only overlap three working hours in a day." We often find that solutions implemented to solve distance problems, like e-mail, are used ineffectively to work across time zones and vice versa, resulting in work delays due to longer response times. It is precisely this correlation between spatial and temporal separation (i.e., time separated sites are usually far apart in distance) that makes studying the effects of time zones difficult to tease out.

To better accentuate the differences between distance and time separation, we provide a comparison chart (fig. 10-3). One key distinguishing factor between distance and time is that the effects of spatial distance are mostly symmetrical in that the distance between two team members is the same for both members. In contrast, the effects of temporal distance are asymmetrical in that one individual's work schedule is ahead while the other one's is behind a given number of hours. This is not a minor difference because it affects workflow sequence, as in the case of Follow-the-Sun.

Issue	Distance/spatial	Time/temporal
Symmetry	Symmetric: $\text{dist}(A \to B) = \text{dist}(B \leftarrow A)$	Asymmetric: $\text{time}(A \to B) \neq \text{time}(B \leftarrow A)$
Workflow	Timing/sequence less critical	Timing/sequence more important
Measure	Physical distance, travel time	Hours apart, work time overlap
Dispersion	Once separated, you are separated, regardless of distance	Effects are more pronounced as the number of sites and the time zone span increases
The Impact of Technology	More easily bridged	More difficult to bridge, temporal separation changes patterns of interaction (alternating between synchronous and asynchronous)
Communication choice	Choice between async or sync any time	During async periods, choice between async technology or waiting for the overlap period to communicate synchronously

Figure 10-3: Difference between time and distance separation.

In addition, how time separation affects delay depends on the timing of the workflow. Of course, with time separation, urgent matters are more likely to be delayed until the next day to be resolved. Meanwhile, pure distance separation can be mitigated with technology such as the telephone, e-mail, texting, or videoconferencing, thereby helping reduce delay.

The nature of the task

The type of task matters when coordinating work across time zones. For example, the workflow in certain tasks, such as in software testing tasks, can be structured and carried out sequentially (e.g., Follow-the-Sun). Other tasks, like decision-making tasks, require more spontaneous interaction, so time zones get in the way. Yet, other tasks can be partitioned into independent components that can be carried out from just about any location. We discuss key task characteristics that affect coordination across time zones.

- *Task structure*—some tasks are very structured (e.g., processing a mortgage application), some are unstructured (e.g., developing a strategic plan), and others are somewhere in between (e.g., developing software). Structured tasks can be coordinated more mechanistically with things like schedules, plans, and procedures, so they are less affected by time zone differences. Unstructured tasks generally require a lot of organic communication to share knowledge and coordinate activities, and they are more affected by time zone differences.

- *Time pressure*—while some tasks have time-to-market or other time pressures (e.g., mobile phone feature design), others are given long timelines and are not as affected by time pressures (e.g., enterprise architecture). Overall, time zone differences *increase* task delay, so time sensitive tasks are more affected by time zone differences.

- *Complexity*—simpler tasks are more easily structured and distributed among participants in multiple sites with the necessary batched instructions to complete the task. More complex tasks are harder to distribute across time zones and require more interaction to get the job done.

- *Equivocality*—some tasks are well defined (e.g., assemble widgets) and others are more equivocal (e.g., find the best candidate for a job). An equivocal task is one that has no clear-cut solution and may have many possible paths that lead to a particular solution. Equivocal tasks are more affected by time zone differences because they require substantial communication for convergence of meaning.

What Insight Has Theory Provided?

WHILE COORDINATION THEORY is fairly mature, the collaboration context has changed with dispersion enabled by technology. This has made researchers re-think the applicability of coordination theory to today's modern work environments. Theory shines light on the need for mechanistic and implicit coordination in time-separated collaborations to make up for the limited communication. Our collective research suggests the right mix is some qualified balance between the three coordination types. This means rigorous mechanistic coordination in concert with strong implicit coordination, augmented by organic coordination. Theory also dissects the times when collaborators need to synchronize, for convergence, and when they don't. Finally, theory illuminates the connection between dependencies and outcomes.

EPILOGUE

Future Time

Future Time

TIME ZONES WILL NOT STAND STILL. As we look into the medium-term future of five to fifteen years, we see some factors that affect time zone work as evolving, while other factors will not change. We examine the future of time zones analytically using a Future Studies' "sources of change" framework. We point to two significant sources of change that will be evolving—technology and population.

The first source of change, technology, will facilitate and make easier two components of time zone coordination. "Where do we meet?" will be much easier. People will meet via richer technologies: 3D, virtual worlds, holography and other immersive technologies, all via wireless everywhere. And "When is the best time to meet?" will be an easier question to answer. The tools for syncing meeting times will be more common, better designed into scheduling software and calendars. As of this writing, great strides have already been made in improving the features for these scheduling tools. Another class of tools, awareness technologies, will become ever more invasive, allowing timeshifters to sync at just the right open moment, for example, to catch Thùy when she has ten minutes while waiting in the queue to pick up her five-year-old son.

The second source of change is population. The number of knowledge workers working globally will continue to grow by millions, meaning that many more will be working digitally, needing to collaborate and coordinate around the globe. It is likely that there will be many more millions of global workers working scattertime. Consequently, time zones will become even more important than they are today.

As mentioned, some factors will not evolve. Human biology will not be altered during this time horizon—not yet. Humans will still need to sleep. Workers will still prefer to work during the daytime hours. Knowledge workers' need to coordinate will not go away. While some tasks will be routinized, there will still be countless unstructured slices of work that are slightly ambiguous or require trust to converge with other workers. The reasons for why we need to sync will be just as strong as they are today.

Nevertheless, organizations will mature in their use of time zones. The number of 24-hour organizations will increase. Organizations will leverage time zones more routinely at tactical and strategic levels. They will be more likely to choose Follow-the-Sun and Round-the-Clock strategies, particularly in environments where time-to-market and 24-hour coverage are critical. Organizations will become better at overlaps and handoffs. The Sutherland example from chapter 6 illustrated how a process is carefully sliced into multiple pieces based on resource and time zone; it will become more common for organizations to follow strategies similar to this one.

The impact on the nature of work will be profound. The traditional "9 to 5" work schedule will continue to erode. With millions of workers in scattertime, the *pact* between employer and employee that we described in chapter 7 will be the source of many clashes. In some organizations the pact may evolve into a Time Zone Bill of Rights. Labor unions will become more involved in time zone issues. In parallel, *microsourcing*, the sourcing to small firms and to freelancers will be more common (there are already several million global freelancers offering their labor from near and far via the Internet).

Time zones will also appear as a backdrop in global politics. A harbinger of this is the stream of critical scholarship on time zones that is a variant of the anti-colonial, anti-capitalist, and anti-globalization works that come out of academia, containing polemical titles such as "The gendered time politics of globalization," and passages such as "globalization involves the conflating of 'national time and capitalist time,'" and, "[time is a] quantifiable resource that is open to manipulation, management and control, and subject to commodification, allocation, use and abuse."[146] The interlocking message is that capitalism allows the wealthy to colonize the workers of developing countries into their own time zones.

We opened this book with "Distance is dead, but time zones are not." We do not anticipate that this will change in the next five to fifteen years. There are tactics that a work team can employ to mitigate the effects of time zones (e.g., timeshifting), but these will continue to work with a small number of time zones and shorter time zone spans. Beyond this, the problem is like solving a Rubik's Cube—when you shift one color, other colors fall out of position. Except, that unlike a Rubik's Cube, there is no perfect solution for time zones, only one that is satisficing.

ABOUT

About

Research History and Methodology of the Time Zone Study

E AUTHORS HAVE ALWAYS BEEN time zone challenged. As travelers, immigrants with far-flung families, and as global professionals, we cannot recall when we didn't deal with time zones.

The genesis of our research was in 2002 after Alberto joined Erran at American University in Washington, D.C. We were determined to work together and looked for knowledge gaps in areas that have important applied impact. We spent many afternoons at the whiteboard in Erran's office. We jointly came to the conclusion that time zone separation was the unresolved issue for both research and practice, with profound effects on how work gets done these days.

At this writing, Erran has been studying globally distributed work for about sixteen years, and Alberto for about fourteen years. There is little that we observed that we haven't already seen before. But we bring something new and fresh here—the lens of time zones. It is a lens that has been neglected in both theoretical research and by industry. By using this lens, one sees and understands new problems, new concepts, and new solutions.

From the outset it was clear to us that we should use a multi-method approach to our research in order to understand it thoroughly. Social scientists know that one doesn't really understand a phenomenon unless one uses many tools to examine it. We have used field studies, case studies, surveys, archival data, laboratory experiments, and design science (build–evaluate loop). The only intended method we have not used, yet, is simulation. We plan to do this in the future.

Our main primary research thrusts are noted here:

- **Large company case studies.** We conducted important pieces of our research at firms that opened their doors to us: Intel in 2004-06 and Infosys in 2005. The studies at Intel were conducted using surveys. The study at Infosys was conducted using field interviews. (The Intel study is in Cummings, et al., 2009; and the Infosys study is in Carmel, 2006).
- **Country study.** Conducted in Brazil in 2010. The study included forty-six interviews in fifteen companies. (Carmel and Prikladnicki, 2010).

- **Experimental research.** Conducted on the campus of American University, the University of Michigan, and the University of Oklahoma in 2006-10. We facilitated 246 student subjects in our laboratories in a 3x4 factorial design. (Nan, et al., 2009).
- **Design science.** Our research on Follow-the-Sun, in 2007-2010, was part conceptual and part design science/comparative field study. We not only observed the phenomenon, but also worked in a utilitarian sense on a build–evaluate loop. (Design science seeks to create new and innovative artifacts and methods.) With Yael Dubinsky, we facilitated thirty engineering students during two semesters at the Israel Institute of Technology (Carmel, et al., 2010).
- **Interviews.** We conducted at least twenty-one planned interviews at firms around the world. We also mined our other past and current research projects on global work. Research on shift work was conducted through semi-structured interviews with various knowledge workers during 2008-11.
- **Heard on the street.** We also listen to people everywhere—in workshops we gave, in our classes, in opportunistic chats. Everyone has time zone anecdotes and time zone opinions. Many of these anecdotes and opinions continue to be useful in forming our world view on the wicked problem of time zone coordination.

Use of Names

INDUSTRY PEOPLE ARE CAUTIOUS about any story; consequently, some of the names in this book are aliases in order to protect the identity of the individual or the firm. In many cases small details were also changed so that the reader cannot guess. This is standard procedure in our world. We commit to anonymity unless the source gives us specific permission. The following company names are aliases: Agile Factori, Maryland Bank, CLX, RemCo, KyleSystems, ChromatCity, Axtended. The IBMer Frank Li, mentioned several times, is real, but his name is not.

Author Biographies

ERRAN CARMEL STUDIES THE GLOBALIZATION of technology work, including global teams, offshoring of information technology, new kinds of global sourcing, and the emergence of software industries around the world. He has written two previous books. His 1999 book, "Global Software Teams," was the first on this topic and is considered a landmark in the field,

Espinosa (left) and Carmel (right) outside their offices at American University, Washington, D.C.

helping many organizations take their first steps into distributed technology work. His second book, "Offshoring Information Technology," came out in 2005 and became a required textbook for many courses on outsourcing and offshoring. It is now in its fifth printing. Carmel began his career as a programmer and then project manager. He received his Ph.D., in Management Information Systems from the University of Arizona; his MBA from the University of California at Los Angeles (UCLA), and his B.A. from the University of California at Berkeley. He grew up in Haifa, Israel.

J. Alberto Espinosa studies coordination and performance in global technical projects across global boundaries. He emphasizes his multiple method approach in his research, including theoretical, lab experiments, qualitative studies and survey methods, but his primary focus is on on-site field studies in large technical organizations. His work has been published in the leading scholarly journals and conference proceedings. He began his career as a design engineer; later he was a senior manager with an international NGO where he designed software applications to support global work. He received his Ph.D. and Master of Science degrees in Information Systems from Carnegie Mellon University, Tepper School of Business; an MBA degree from Texas Tech University; and his B.Sc. in Mechanical Engineering from Pontificia Universidad Catolica, Peru. He grew up in Lima, Peru. After receiving his B.Sc. degree, he worked in Peru for five years before immigrating to the United States.

Acknowledgements

TWO PEOPLE WERE ESPECIALLY INVOLVED in the development of this book during the last two years: Chaoqing Hou and Julia Wang, our Research Assistants at American University, who spent countless hours on research and editing.

Our fellow academics helped us research and learn this field over the years. The Intel study was conducted with Cindy Pickering of Intel. Our experiments were conducted with Ning Nan of the University of Oklahoma. Our Brazil study was conducted with Rafael Prikladnicki of PUCRS in Brazil. The Follow-the-Sun study was done in collaboration with Yael Dubinsky of The Israel Institute of Technology and IBM Research in Haifa, Israel.

Many people in industry were interviewed or assisted in other ways. Felipe Soares and Demetrio Bogowicz at Dell, Ron Karpel at CoolSand, Joe Buggy at Sutherland Global Services, Imran Aftab at TenPearls, Jim Walsh at GlobalLogic.

Many colleagues and friends commented on versions of this book including: Paul Tjia, Michael O'Leary, Bonnie Auslander, Peter Keen, Jennifer Marlow, Julia Gaspar, John Tang, and Mark Clark.

As with any big, important project, we involved family. Erran's father, Eli, made numerous comments on the book draft. Delphine Clegg, Alberto's wife, edited the final draft.

Thank you also to Yoram Kalman and Gloria Mark for permission to reprint "So Where Was I."

We have benefited from several research funding sources. These firms funded aspects of this work: Intel, Infosys, and IBM's Haifa Research Center. In addition, American University's Kogod School of Business, where we teach, and its Center for Information Technology and the Global Economy contributed direct and indirect funding. Funding also came from PUCRS in Brazil.

Erran Carmel & J. Alberto Espinosa
Washington D.C., September 2011

APPENDICES

APPENDIX A
Time Zones in Group Calendars

A man with a watch knows what time it is.
A man with two watches is never sure.

Segal's Law

ROUP CALENDARS ARE ONE OF THE MOST basic coordination techniques across time zones. More formally they fall into the domain of time-and-activity-management.[147] These calendars are embedded in common tools such as Microsoft Outlook, with its more than 300 million users. Distributed groups that do not use these tools are usually asking for trouble. Nevertheless, these tools are tricky, especially if individuals are traveling/moving across time zones. If all individuals stay put and never get on a jet and travel across time zones, then the little kinks that still show up in using group calendars are rather small by now.

There are three settings that affect the scheduling of a meeting for each individual:

- The clock setting inside the individual's computer.
- The local time zone setting inside the individual's computer. This is important when the user is travelling across time zones.
- The Daylight Saving Time (DST) inside the individual's computer.

All three factors must be set correctly on both the meeting organizer's computer and on each attendee's computer, otherwise the correct meeting time will not be reflected on the calendar. In the case of someone traveling across time zones during a project, he or she should make sure that the settings for both the local time and time zone are correct. Users either need to adjust settings manually or set the computer time in sync with the Internet (time.nist.gov).

Adjustment for DST and back is another nuisance. For example, in 2010 the iPhone DST adjustments did not function properly in some U.S. locations and these propagated into one's synchronized calendars. Because of the mismatch, users received calendar notifications on their iPhones earlier or later than what was showing up on their Outlook calendars. When it first happened, not everyone was aware of this problem. As a result, some found themselves waking up an hour later than normal.

The iPhone bug notwithstanding, DST adjustments generally work well and are becoming invisible to users. But even when calendars handle the DST issues correctly, the change can still cause problems for global project teams. Since DST adjustments happen infrequently, people tend to forget about their implications. For instance, an agile software project with teams from California, China and India set their daily meeting at 21:30 California time as part of their daily routine, but no one really sets a notification for meetings. However, when DST kicks-in in the United States someone who is unaware of the time change might miss a meeting.

It is tricky to set meeting times for a *future* time zone. Let's say you are in New York this week and in London the following week, with local meetings in each location. How do you set the calendar meetings? Most calendar tools, such as Google Calendar, support this. When you are in New York, after creating a new event for a meeting in London, you can assign the London time zone for that event. Then the meeting time is correctly reflected under the current calendar time zone of New York time. After traveling to London, you can set the computer's calendar time zone as London; then, all the events will be interpreted using the new (correct) time zone.

The Lotus Notes calendar and other similar calendars have sophisticated features for scheduling meetings across time zones. The calendar allows you to check the availability of the invitees so you can choose the time slot that works best for the whole team. However, watch out for changes in the invitees' availability because of timeshifting. Often the user will not have changed his/her working hours accordingly.

APPENDIX B
Time Zone Fine Points

What time is it where you are?

NO QUESTION ANNOYS INTERNATIONAL employees more than, "What time is it over there?" Finding out is as simple as typing, "What time is it in Hong Kong?" into Google or Bing.

For more detail we use timeanddate.com. It has all the answers and is very reliable. Steffen Thorsen, a young Norwegian, founded it in 1995 and now manages the site full time.

It's easy to remember some time zones, sometimes. Much of East Asia, including all of China, Hong Kong and Singapore, are exactly twelve hours ahead of the U.S. East Coast, including New York City. So, if it is summertime (DST) and you are in one of those two time zones, just flip the a.m. and p.m.

Next, if you are in an Indian-British relationship and you want to know what the time is in the other country, simply turn your watch upside-down! Yes, this really works, though only with analog watches.

Time zone notation

The official standard notation for the time of an event is usually in UTC/GMT with no offset. It looks like this: **2010-06-20 01:48Z,** where Z is UTC/GMT. This format reduces confusion about data format and about time zone offset. It comes from ISO 8601, International Organization for Standardization (ISO) as the international standard for the exchange of date and time-related data.

If you want to write in a helpful time format so your distant colleagues can correctly figure it out, write:

Our voice call is scheduled for

Monday, June 24, 2013 9:15 AM EDT (my local time)

Monday, June 24, 2013 13:15 (UTC/GMT)

Random time zone fun facts

- Stations in Antarctica generally set their clocks to the time of their supply bases.
- Because the earliest and latest time zones are twenty-six hours apart, any given calendar date exists at some point on the globe for fifty hours.
- There are numerous places where three or more time zones meet. One is at the tri-country border of Finland, Norway and Russia.
- The world has forty time zones, not twenty-four as popularly believed.
- The largest time zone gap along a political border is the 3.5-hour gap along the border of China (GMT +8) and Afghanistan (GMT +4:30).
- New Zealand was the first country to standardize its time zone.

APPENDIX C
Time Dispersion Indicators

ECALL THAT IN CHAPTER 2 we introduced the four time zone factors. These are rather simple in and of themselves, but they can be combined to create more powerful indicators of time zone dispersion. Three of these are presented here:

WorkDay Span (WDS): Represents the maximum number of hours of work time per day spanned by the team. This parameter may be a more useful parameter than the time zone span from chapter 2 for some work arrangements like Follow-the-Sun and Round-the-Clock because it provides an indication of how much a workday can be stretched for shift coverage. Using our example (fig. 2-1), in India the workday begins at 02:30 GMT (08:00 local time) and in Washington, D.C. the day ends at 22:30 GMT (17:30 local time), so the workday span is twenty hours. The maximum value of WDS is twenty-four.

Time Zone Overlap Ratio (OR): Computed as the number of hours of work time overlap between sites divided by the total number of work hours in the day. So if there are two sites, New York and Texas, with one time zone separation, there are 8 hours of overlap in a 9-hour workday, which yields 0.89.

This ratio takes a value from 0 (no work time overlap) to 1 (full work time overlap). The ratio for the full team can be computed as a simple average or as a weighted average using the number of team members in each pair of sites as the weighting factor. When adjustments are made for overtime and time shifting as depicted in figure 2-4, then the effective overlap index improves. For example, the overlap ratio between Washington, D.C. and Gurgaon is 0, but if each site shifts its work hours by 2 hours (i.e., Washington, D.C. starts/ends 2 hours earlier and Gurgaon starts/ ends 2 hours later), the effective work time overlap becomes 2.5 hours with an overlap index of $2.5/9 = 0.28$; and if both sites work two hours overtime (and timeshift in the right direction), the overlap ratio increases to $6.5/11 = 0.59$. With three or more different time zones, the OR can be computed as the average of the respective ORs for each pair of time zones. Naturally, this average can be weighted based on the number of people in each time zone, which leads us to the OCOR.

OC Time Zone Overlap Ratio (OCOR): This is the O'Leary and Cummings ratio, hence "OC."[148] The calculation of this ratio is similar to the overlap ratio, above, but takes into account each individual member-to-member pairing. Thus, it measures more accurately how widely scattered, or concentrated, members are across time zones. A team may have a large time zone span over several times zones, but with one large dominant site. Generally speaking, the larger the ratio, the more the team will operate as a co-located team. For instance, in the Washington, D.C.–Haifa–Gurgaon case of figure 2-1, the OR for these three sites is (5.5/9 + 1.5/9 + 0/9)/3 = 0.26, (assuming a nine-hour workday). However, if we consider a team of twenty-three members (i.e., 23 x 22/2 = 253 dyads) operating from these three sites, but with one dominant site having twenty members (Gurgaon), and one member in Haifa and two in Washington, D.C., this yields an OCOR ratio of 0.80, which is dramatically higher than the OR of 0.26 above.[149]

An improvement on the OCOR (or the more general OR) is to include a measure for each dyad's actual dependency. After all, some dyads may never need to interact and others may interact infrequently. The dyad's dependency can be measured with survey questionnaires or communication frequency scores and, naturally, the ratio computations become more complicated, but more meaningful. A simpler approach is to weight by using only a binary: 1, if the dyad collaborates in the task; and 0, if it doesn't.

APPENDIX D
So Where Was I?

CHAPTER 9 INTRODUCED the science of interruptions. This appendix is an interview on workplace interruptions with Gloria Mark of the University of California at Irvine. This interview originally appeared in *Information Overload Forum* in 2008 and appears here verbatim with permission of the author and interviewee.

[Excerpted Article Begins:] Before reading this interview, ask yourself these three questions: How many times are you interrupted in a typical workday? How long does it take you to get back on task once you are interrupted? And, who is the one person who interrupts you the most in a typical workday? Jot down the answers, and see how your guesses relate to Dr. Mark's fascinating findings. Prepare to be surprised!

What are interruptions?

Dr. Mark started by explaining the important distinction between external and internal interruptions. External interruptions are probably what everyone thinks of when hearing the term "workplace interruptions": these are situations when someone or something makes us stop the work we are doing. The three most common categories of external interruptions are someone who steps into the room where we are working, e-mail notifications that alert us to an incoming message, and a phone that rings. And, what are internal interruptions? These are situations in which we stop the work we are doing with no apparent external cause. The two most common examples are getting up to leave the room we are working in, and stopping the work we are doing to check the computer for incoming messages. As Dr. Mark made this distinction, I glanced at my own screen, and saw that the little white envelope was already in my system tray... Will I dare check my e-mail?

The answers to the three questions

I had no time to check my e-mail since my attention was drawn to Dr. Mark's description of how, through careful observations and measurements, she and her colleagues discovered that a whopping 44% of all interruptions people experience in the workplace are internal interruptions! Moreover, they found that the knowledge workers they closely tracked for hundreds and hundreds of hours were interrupted or switched the topic they were working on almost every 11 minutes! Indeed, even these blocks of 11 minutes were broken down into short tasks that lasted, on average, only 3 minutes before they were abandoned. Lastly, the research showed that on average it took people more than 20 minutes to get back to the task they were on when they were interrupted. Given these findings, is it any wonder that Dr. Mark's 2004 paper with Victor Gonzales was titled: "Constant, Constant, Multi-tasking Craziness"? How do we get *anything* done?

Interruptions and Information Overload

Just as Dr. Mark started explaining the link between Information Overload and workplace interruptions, I heard her phone ringing. I tried to ignore it but the Skype call we were on was very clear and it sounded as if the phone on my desk were ringing. I smiled to myself: there was our first interruption.

Dr. Mark bravely ignored the ringing phone, and continued describing an experiment in which they induced two types of interruptions on the participants: the interruptions were either 1) related to the topic the person was working on or 2) they were not related to the topic. The hypothesis was that interruptions which were not related to the topic at hand would cause more information overload than those interruptions that were related to the topic

Just as Dr. Mark started describing the unexpected findings, her cell phone started ringing. This time we both agreed that it sounded like she should answer the call. And to be honest, I used the opportunity to check my e-mail. Dr. Mark returned and continued describing the surprise of finding that in actuality, people who were interrupted performed just as well as those who were not. Not only did they not perform more poorly but they actually completed the task faster. It looked as if people compensated for the interruptions by being more efficient. Nevertheless, the interruptions did have an impact: they led to significantly increased levels of stress, frustration, time pressure and effort. And this, Dr. Mark emphasizes, is the overload we experience.

Good interruptions?

So, are all interruptions bad? Not necessarily says Dr. Mark. Some interruptions, for example, have a social function. If you are working by yourself, you have a need to communicate with other people and... RING RING RING now it was my phone ringing, and both of us started laughing. My son answered the phone on another extension, but just as Dr. Mark started describing a new study they just completed, he stepped into my study and handed me the phone. Another few seconds, and I was back with Dr. Mark and the new study. So, where were we? Ah, yes, in the study they found that when people interrupt themselves and take a break, quite often they use the break to browse social networking sites and blogs. Dr. Mark's interpretation is that this might be a new type of work break where, instead of going to the coffee room or getting up and walking around, people interact socially online. Dr. Mark's conclusion is that interruptions are sometimes very beneficial: they are opportunities for some social interaction, they can help trigger new ideas, or they could be used to "incubate" problems for a while. For example, programmers might leave a programming problem alone for a while, do something else, and then get back to the problem and find a better solution to it.

An addict getting her fix on the sidewalk in Berlin

Despite some benefits, interruptions are usually negative. Several years ago Dr. Mark was on sabbatical in Berlin. It was during the World Cup and, probably because of the heavy user load, the ISP she was using was down for two weeks. In these two weeks offline, she was able to finish writing a paper that she had been trying to complete for months. The fact that she was offline and not constantly interrupted by the need to check and respond to e-mails made all the difference. The part I won't forget about this story is how every night at around 10 p.m., Dr. Mark would walk up to a travel agency that had a hotspot, sit on the stairs in front of the closed door, and go online, despite the astonished looks of passers-by who were wondering why this woman was sitting in the middle of a busy street with her laptop.

Is such an "Internet fast" the solution to interruptions? Not according to Dr. Mark's personal experience. She told me that she tried repeating the experience and going offline for periods of time but that she was not able to repeat her successful Internet "holiday." The only weapon she has successfully adopted against information overload is not using IM, mainly since when she did turn her IM on, many students chose that method to contact her and the level of interruption was just too high.

So what did we have?

During this 30 minute interview we had two phone calls, one cell phone call, and one person stepping into the room. I also checked my e-mail once. I think that given the study findings, only four interruptions in 30 minutes is pretty good! Did you too manage to read this whole interview without interruptions?

End Notes

1   Some of the content in this prologue is based on *Hidden Rhythms: Schedules and Calendars in Social Life* by Eviatar Zerubavel, 1985. The calendar is interesting to our topic because it was synchronized globally well before the synchronization of time zones. The global standard that emerged is the one used today: the Gregorian calendar. Its roots are in the Catholic world. Beginning in the 1700s, the Gregorian calendar was adopted by most of non-Catholic Europe, including Norway, Denmark, and all the German and Dutch Protestant states. In the late 1800s, Japan and Egypt became the first non-Christian countries to adopt the Gregorian calendar. By World War I, other newly emerging countries followed suit. China adopted the calendar after the Chinese Revolution of 1912.

2   From Norgate (2006) and Barnett (1998).

3   Heejin and Liebenau (2000).

4   Carmel and Tjia (2005).

5   Dennis, Fuller, et al. (2008).

6   Lu, Wynn, et al. (2003).

7   Working Mother (2009).

8   A useful summary of weekends around the world can be found online at: http://en.wikipedia.org/wiki/Workweek_and_weekend

9   Weekends in Palestine's two regions are different. The Hamas-dominated Gaza region weekend it is Thursday-Friday, while in the Fatah-dominated West Bank region it is Friday-Saturday.

10 Segalla (2011).

11 This "fast, fast, fast" trend in society has led to some interesting contra-trends like the "slow" movement (and even—we are serious—the World Institute of Slowness).

12 European and US shiftwork statistics comes from three sources: McMenamin and Terence (2007); Eurostat (2010); Costa (1996).

13 UBS is a global financial firm. The data are from Norgate (2006).

14 McMenamin (2007); Also see chapter 3. Separately, we professors note that academics have worked in this fashion for a long time. It is not uncommon to find a professor working at home on a research paper at 02:00 on a Saturday and then taking Tuesday afternoon off to go to a ballgame.

15 Westernholz uses interesting but different terms for scattertime, *task timers*, and differentiates between 'clock timers' (with rigid working times and a clear distinction between work and leisure) and 'task timers.' Westenholz (2006).

16 Economist (2008).

17 The study used data from 1975 and 1995 and most respondents were still working "from 9 to 5." Breedveld (2008).

18 There are many scheduling and project tools. At this writing, we see buzz on tungle.me. Computerworld surveyed twenty free and low-cost tools to "help your team work together" in "Online collaboration on the cheap:"

http://www.computerworld.com/s/article/9177575/Online_collaboration_on_the_cheap_20_free_ and_low_cost_tools

[19] The power to meet at your convenience. One often hears the lament that, "We always have to schedule at a time that is convenient to the Americans." The less powerful are the ones that timeshift more dramatically. In India, while higher paid software engineers work the day shift, call center workers are required to timeshift. The busy call center shift in India begins at 17:00. In relatively wealthier Brazil, the picture is the same. In our Brazilian study, we found that generally, the Brazilian sites are the ones that timeshifted to align to the headquarters/center in other countries, or to the clients' hours. Isolates, those smaller nodes often made up of just a single individual, tend to timeshift the most.

[20] Segalla (2010).

[21] Microsoft Vista project of 2008 used rotating timeslot meetings to share the pain. Described in Bird, et al. (2009).

[22] Yet, there are different settings, such as the open source environment studied by Colazo, where he found, rather surprisingly, that more time zone dispersed projects are more productive, but offered no explanation. Colazo (2008).

[23] Nan, Espinosa, et al. (2009).

[24] Cummings, Espinosa, et al. (2009).

[25] Siebdrat, Hoegl, et al. (2009).

[26] O'Leary and Cummings (2007).

[27] Brooks (1995).

[28] Herbsleb and Mockus (2003).

[29] Gopal, Espinosa, et al. (2011).

[30] Espinosa and Pickering (2006).

[31] The punch clock was invented by a New York jeweler in the 1880s. The device became ubiquitous in manufacturing facilities and, within a few decades, most were made by the International Time Recording Company, which eventually became IBM.

[32] Timeshifting even takes place in agile software development, which at first was in denial even about distributed work, cf. Miller (2009).

[33] With some recent exceptions, such as Tang, Chen, et al. (2011).

[34] Case background for Coolsand Technologies: Based in Beijing, this enterprise designs chips for mobile communications and multimedia. In 2008, at the time of this case, it had about 300 employees. The System on a Chip is marketed to the hypercompetitive mobile phone market. Therefore, Coolsand is in a product vertical in which speed, or, time-to-market, is one of the most intense of any product category in the world. As the CTO says, "We are always in a hurry; everything is always urgent." The company was founded in 2002 by experienced engineers who had met and worked together in Silicon Valley.

[35] Technology used at Coolsand: The main work platform in use across sites was the Cadence Encounter, a CAD platform. This meant that the firm's digital objects were all checked into a common area. Furthermore, many of the standards enforced by using the common Cadence package tend to simplify communication between sites. The firm also collaborated by using the SVN version control system. The popular chat tool was MSN.

36 It is unfortunate that this important concept of handoff between shifts is not broadly recognized. Part of the problem may be jargon. We have noticed many names for handoff. Some call it a turnover meeting. In a Japanese software collaboration, the one-hour overlap was referred to as "shake off." When we did time zone research with Professor Dubinsky and her students in Israel, they started calling the handoff "passing the baton."

37 The language of shifts is adapted from Monk and Folkard (1992).

38 Coleman (1995).

39 Lister (2010).

40 Tang, Chen, et al. (2011).

41 Should the liaison be the only channel of communication across time zones? One school of thought, voiced by Jim Walsh, CTO of GlobalLogic, a global software firm, is that only the temporal liaisons should be overlapping between the two distant sites. He argues, "you want to minimize real-time touch points," because engineers are not naturally good communicators, and to create many touch points is to create a recipe for problems. Therefore, during the formalized handoff, only one liaison from each site is involved in the handoff. Note that these liaisons are chosen based on the quality of their communications skills.

42 Miller (2009).

43 On MBWA/MBFA/MBTA: MBWA was first publicized by HP's David Packard in the 1940s and revived due to the highly influential book "In Search of Excellence." With the dawn of virtual organizations in the 1990s, most observers, including us, generally believed that the dominant work configuration was that of clustered locations in which co-located programmers work together in one office and managers would fly from location to location in order to meet with their programmers; see Carmel (2010).

44 Sagi (2005).

45 Baker, Ferguson, et al. (2003).

46 Coleman (1995).

47 Craig (2008).

48 Two pointers on this: Grinter, Herbsleb, et al. (1999); Carmel (1999).

49 Regarding agile across time zones: From a technical point of view, this notion of continuous integration and continuous delivery means that there are regular, sometimes daily, software "builds" that serve to improve the feedback loop. There is also a lot of test automation/test-driven development that reduces the need for synchronous communication. Team members in well-managed, agile projects tend to pay more attention to project awareness indicators, informing all the individual players about what everybody else is doing.

50 Intel case project data: This was a business application project for budget resource allocation. Business users, requirements analysts and software developers collaborated on this project. Porting of the application was made possible using a company in Russia to move from Access to a web-based application (app) using SQL. Locations involved were: Bangalore, India; Dublin, Ireland; Israel; Swindon, United Kingdom; Nizny Novgorod, Russia; Cavite, the Philippines; Shanghai, China; and in the United States: Arizona; Folsom/Santa Clara, California, and Portland, Oregon. Duration of the project was about nine months. This case was co-authored with Cynthia Pickering from Intel Corporation.

51 Technologies used by the Intel team: The team also relied heavily on communication technologies like instant messenger for short questions, electronic mail for longer questions, phone and collaboration

tools like desktop sharing for discussions that required direct interaction, and workflow tools like share content repositories and project coordination for more structured information sharing. The focus of the communication seemed to be around task awareness or knowing "who is doing what" at any given time so that inquiries could be directed to the right people.

52 Tang, Chen, et al. (2011).

53 Carmel and Prikladnicki (2010).

54 Longitude matters. Economists Stein and Daude argue that longitude matters! Using bilateral Foreign Direct Investment (FDI) data, they found that time zone separation has a negative effect on the location of FDI. This is interesting because economists have consistently showed that geographic distance matters in economic activity. They also found that the impact of time zones is increasing. Stein and Daude (2007).

55 The concept of modularity is fundamental in all engineering disciplines, allowing a small work object like a software program to be intellectually manageable. *Information hiding,* introduced by Parnas Parnas (1972), is a general design concept that calls for properly structuring the software's modules so that the design logic is hidden from its user, the programmer. If the programmer has to comprehend less design logic, less of the big picture, then the need for coordination with other programmers' modules can be reduced. Distant sites can choose along a continuum of coupling and time zone separation in order to minimize coupling between time zones.

56 Two pointers on this: Grinter, Herbsleb, et al. (1999); Carmel (1999).

57 Segalla (2010).

58 Seasonal time zone chart does not reflect short transition periods in spring and fall seasons.

59 Barrett (2009).

60 Lacity, Carmel, et al. (2011).

61 Carmel and Abbott (2006).

62 Winter hours in Northern Hemisphere; summer hours, including DST, in the Southern Hemisphere.

63 Vijayan (1996).

64 Carmel and Eisenberg (2005).

65 Brazilian branding appears in Dinnie (2007).

66 Carmel and Prikladnicki (2010). This section of the research received assistance from Rafael Audy Glanzner and Estevão Ricardo Hess.

67 Several pages are devoted to time proximity in the colorful, in-depth 2009 report of the Brazilian IT association Brasscom. Brasscom (2009).

68 Carmel (1999).

69 Boudreau (2005) in the *San Jose Mercury News.*

70 In our 2010 article we formally defined Follow-the-Sun: *A round-the-clock work rotation method aimed at reducing project duration, in which the knowledge product is owned and advanced by a production site and is then handed-off at the end of each workday to the next production site several time-zones west.* Carmel, Espinosa, et al. (2010).

71 On Follow-the-Sun, astute observers tend to ask: So, why not locate all three teams, instead of all over the globe, in the same location? All three teams could be working on the same shift in the same location. The framer of this question assumes that labor is perfectly interchangeable and its price is irrelevant. Both of

these are far from true in the real world. In addition, for years it has been known from Brooks and others that larger teams have intra-team coordination overhead, whereas three small teams working sequentially can reduce the intra-team coordination.

72   Carmel (1999).

73   Smith and Reinersten (1991).

74   Carmel, Espinosa, et al. (2010).

75   Cummings, Espinosa, et al. (2009).

76   Nan, Espinosa, et al. (2009).

77   Carmel (2006).

78   Cameron (2004).

79   With time boxing, the cycle time is fixed and, if there are delays, the deliverables for that cycle are adjusted, not the deadline.

80   Dubinsky and Carmel (2009).

81   Carmel, Espinosa, et al. (2010).

82   When Round-the-Clock services are outsourced, as they often are, the outsourcing provider can deliver services through one of two possible models. In the first, the outsourcing provider gives the client dedicated service such as five customer support representatives entirely devoted to the customer, whether or not any calls come in. The second is that the outsourcing provider delivers shared services, somewhat like a doctor's nighttime answering service where the representatives are shared.

83   Regarding the work of uTest: In the same vein as outsourcing, we call this microsourcing, where the sourcing units are very small. It is often one person working solo in his apartment.

84   Mirchandani (2003). Other critics of time colonialism are in the book edited by Hassan and Purser (2007).

85   Carmel (2006).

86   On shift design and transportation: If taxis are involved, then shift designers need to keep in mind the taxi routing schedule since every taxi can only take up to four people. Thus, the company needs to spread out pickups and drop-offs.

87   On the topic of company–provided meals for employees working evening/night shifts one tech manager related: "we don't give them a heavy meal otherwise they may fall asleep."

88   The implicit pact that we describe here is sometimes known as the *psychological contract*, the mutual beliefs and informal obligations between an employer and an employee.

89   The "build" dashboard at Agile Factori is a continuous integration tool from Hudson. It is a FOSS tool.

90   The topic of health risks from night shift is compiled from the following sources: Monk and Folkard (1992); Foster and Kreitzman (2005); Costa (1996); Mandel (2005); Freehling (2007).

91   Bureau of Labor Statistics (2007). U.S. Department of Labor, 2007.

92   Mandel (2005).

93   Long working hours and sleep disturbances: the Whitehall II prospective cohort study. Virtanen, Ferrie, et al. (2009).

94   Mandel (2005).

95   Barley, Mayerson, et al. (2011).

96   Southernton (2003).

[97] Kuper and Marmot (2003).

[98] Mercer (2009).

[99] Foster and Kreitzman (2005).

[100] Norgate (2006).

[101] Body temperature chart is from Coleman (1995) and page 9 of Monk and Folkard (1992).

[102] Foster and Kreitzman (2005).

[103] Foster and Kreitzman (2005).

[104] Even a little bit out of the rhythm is hard: NASA scientists working on the Mars daily cycle of 24.7 hours quickly got into jet lag in spite of the small difference. Thompson (2008).

[105] Foster and Kreitzman (2005).

[106] Melatonin, a natural hormone that can be purchased in most countries, is commonly used as a jetlag drug. At dusk, as the light begins to weaken, the brain's pineal gland begins to produce the hormone melatonin, continuing during the night until there is light the next day. This hormone affects the modulation of wake/sleep patterns. The studies are somewhat inconclusive about the perfect way to take Melatonin, though in general it should be taken before you go to sleep.

[107] Foster and Kreitzman (2005).

[108] Coleman (1995).

[109] International Labor Organisation (1990). Note that date of coming into force was 1995.

[110] The narratives at the beginning of chapter 9 are synthetic narratives.

[111] Zerubavel (1985).

[112] Zerubavel (1985).

[113] Palmer (2011).

[114] Hancock, Vercruyssen, et al. (1992).

[115] Blatchley, Dixon, et al. (2007).

[116] Horne, Brass C., et al. (1980).

[117] Foster and Kreitzman (2005).

[118] Gersick (1988).

[119] Claessens, van Eerde, et al. (2007).

[120] We surveyed cross-cultural differences in chapter 9 of Carmel and Tjia (2005).

[121] Levine (1997).

[122] On matching time styles and tasks: Carol Saunders and colleagues suggest looking at people's time styles and matching them with compatible tasks so those who come from linear cultures are offered tasks that involve production or scheduling, while people from elastic cultures are offered tasks that tend to have more interruptions. Saunders, Vogel et al. (2004).

[123] Hall (1959).

[124] Levine (1997).

[125] Setting up Quiet Time as an antidote to timeshifting also begs the question, "How much time do individuals really communicate during overlap time?" Without getting into these details, we contend that it is the importance of the interaction and not its quantity or duration that matters.

[126] Mark, González, et al. (2005).

127 Richtel (2010).

128 Mark, González, et al. (2005).

129 Some thoughtful researchers have even made it their mission to study interruptions and have formed the Information Overload research group. http://www.iorgforum.org/

130 Boulton (2008).

131 Richtel (2010).

132 Gumm (2007).

133 Teasley (2000).

134 Mechanistic is also referred to as coordination by plan, by program or impersonal. Organic coordination is also referred to as coordination by feedback or by mutual adjustment. Implicit coordination is also referred to as cognitive coordination.

135 March & Simon (1958).

136 Wittenbaum & Stasser (1996).

137 Situation awareness involves the perception of events in the task environment, the comprehension about the meaning of the event relative to the task, and the projection of how this event will affect future states of the task. Endsley (1995).

138 Cooke, et al. (2000).

139 Kraut & Streeter (1995).

140 This is a "new" theory that has not yet been tested empirically. Dennis, et al. (2008).

141 Gumm (2007).

142 Three important types of coordination in technical work are: technical—some individual parts of the final product don't work well together; temporal—some tasks in the project are not ready when they are supposed to be, delaying others in the team; and, process—there are many instances of priority conflicts, not following established procedures, escalation issues, etc.

143 Allen (1977).

144 Cummings (2004).

145 Cummings, et al. (2009).

146 Some of the titles are from: Mirchandani (2003), Adam (2002), Sassen (2000). "The gendered time politics" is from Sassen (2000); "quantifiable resource that is open to manipulation" is from Adam (1998).

147 Dyson (2005).

148 O'Leary and Cummings (2007).

149 (20 x 19)/2 = 190 dyads within Bangalore (overlap ratio of 1.0); 1 dyad within Washington, D.C. (overlap ratio of 1.0); 0 dyads within Bangalore; 20 dyads between Bangalore and Haifa (overlap ratio of 5.5/9 = 0.61); 40 dyads between Washington, D.C. and Bangalore (overlap ratio of 0) and 2 dyads between Washington, D.C. and Haifa (overlap ratio of 1.5/9 = 0.17); resulting in an OC overlap ratio of (190x1.0 + 1x1.0 + 0x1.0 + 20x0.61 + 40x0 + 2x0.17)/253 = 0.80.

References

Adam, B. (2002). The Gendered Time Politics of Globalization: Of Shadowlands and Elusive Justice. *Feminist Review, 70*, 2-29.

Allen, T. J. (1977). *Managing the Flow of Technology*. Cambridge, MA: MIT Press.

BAITOCC. (2010). *Brazil IT-BPO Book 2008-2009*.

Baker, A., Ferguson, S., & Dawson, D. (2003). The Perceived Value of Time Controls Versus Shiftworkers. *Time & Society, 12*(1), 27–39.

Barley, S. R., Meyerson, D. E., & Grodal, S. (2011). E-Mail as Source and Symbol of Stress. *Organization Science, 22*(4), 887-906.

Barnett, J. E. (1998). *Time's Pendulum: From Sundials to Atomic Clocks, the Fascinating History of Timekeeping and How Our Discoveries Changed the World*. Basic Books.

Barrett, A. (2009, February 13). Costa Rica: Cultural Similarities Make It an Outsourcing Favorite. *Businessweek*.

Bird, C., Devanbu, P., Gall, H., & Murphy, B. (2009). Does Distributed Development Affect Software Quality? An Empirical Case Study of Windows Vista, Research Highlights. *Communications of the Association for Computer Machinery (CACM), 52*(8).

Blatchley, B., Dixon, R., Purvis, A., Slack, J., Thomas, T., Weber, N., et al. (2007). Computer Use and the Perception of Time. *North American Journal of Psychology*.

Boudreau, J. (2005, December 19). Valley Start-Ups' Cubicles Thousands of Miles Apart. *SilconValley.com*.

Boulton, C. (2008, January 3). Collaboration: The $588 Billion Problem. *eWEEK*.

Breedveld, K. (2008). The Double Myth of Flexibilization: Trends in Scattered Work Hours, and Differences in Time-Sovereignty. *Time & Society*.

Brooks, F. (1995). *The Mythical Man-Month: Essays on Software Engineering* (Anniversary ed.). Reading, MA: A. Wesley.

Cameron, A. (2004). A Novel Approach to Distributed Concurrent Software Development Using A "Follow-the-Sun" Technique. Unpublished EDS working paper.

Carmel, E. (1999). *Global Software Teams: Collaborating across Borders and Time Zones*. Prentice Hall.

Carmel, E. (2010). MBTA: Management by Timeshifting Around. In D. Smite, N. B. Moe & P. J. Ågerfalk (Eds.), *Agility across Time and Space: Implementing Agile Methods in Global Software Projects*: Springer.

Carmel, E., & Abbott, P. (2007). Why Nearshore Means That Distance Matters. *Communications of the Association for Computer Machinery (CACM)*.

Carmel, E., & Eisenberg, J. (2006). Narratives That Software Nations Tell Themselves. *Communications of the Association for Information Systems (CAIS), 17*(39).

Carmel, E., & Prikladnicki, R. (July 22 2010). Does Time Zone Proximity Matter for Brazil? A Study of the Brazilian IT Industry *Social Science Research Network*.

Carmel, E., & Tjia, P. (2005). *Offshoring Information Technology: Sourcing and Outsourcing to a Global Workforce*: Cambridge University Press.

References

Claessens, B. J. C., Eerde, W. v., Rutte, C. G., & Roe, R. A. (2007). A Review of the Time Management Literature. *Personnel Review, 36*(2), 255-276.

Colazo, J. (2008). *Following the Sun: Exploring Productivity in Temporally Dispersed Teams.* Paper presented at the Americas Conference on Information Systems (AMCIS Proceedings).

Coleman, R. M. (1995). *The 24 Hour Business: Maximizing Productivity through Round-the-Clock Operations:* Amacom.

Cooke, N. J., Salas, E., Cannon-Bowers, J. A., & Stout, R. J. (2000). Measuring Team Knowledge. *Human Factors, 42*(1), 151-173.

Costa, G. (1996). The Impact of Shift and Night Work on Health. *Applied Ergonomics.*

Craig, A. (2008, July 5). Piper Alpha Survivor Recalls Sea Disaster. *Newcastle Evening Chronicle.*

Cummings, J. (2004). Work Groups, Structural Diversity, and Knowledge Sharing in a Global Organization. *Managment Science, 50*(3), 352-364.

Cummings, J., Espinosa, J. A., & Pickering, C. (2009). Crossing Spatial and Temporal Boundaries in Globally Distributed Projects: A Relational Model of Coordination Delay. *Information Systems Research, 20*(3), 420-439.

Dennis, A. R., Fuller, R. M., & Valacich, J. S. (2008). Media, Tasks, and Communication Processes: A Theory of Media Synchronicity. *MIS Quarterly, 32*(3), 575-600.

Dinnie, K. (2007). *Nation Branding: Concepts, Issues, Practice:* Butterworth-Heinemann.

Dubinsky, Y., & Carmel, E. (2009). *Passing the Baton: Eclipse Plug-in to Enhance Coordination in Distributed Teams.* Paper presented at the 31th International Conference of Software Engineering (ICSE proceedings), Vancouver, Canada.

Dyson, E. (2005). When 2.0: Time and Timing. *Release 1.0 Newsletter, 24*(2).

Economist. (2008, April 10). A Survey of Mobility: Nomads at Last. *The Economist.*

Endsley, M. (1995). Toward a Theory of Situation Awareness in Dynamic Systems. *Human Factors, 37*(1).

Espinosa, J. A., & Carmel, E. (2004). The Impact of Time Separation on Coordination in Global Software Teams: A Conceptual Foundation. *Journal of Software Process: Practice and Improvement, 8*(4), 249-266.

Espinosa, J. A., & Pickering, C. (2006). *The Effect of Time Separation on Coordination Processes and Outcomes: A Case Study.* Paper presented at the 39th Hawaiian International Conference on System Sciences, Poipu, Kauai, Hawaii.

Espinosa, J. A., Slaughter, S. A., Kraut, R. E., & Herbsleb, J. D. (2007). Team Knowledge and Coordination in Geographically Distributed Software Development. *Journal of Management Information Systems, 24*(1), 135-169.

Eurostat. (2011). Employees Working on Shift Work as a Percentage of the Total of Employees for a Given Sex and Age Group (%). from Eurostat European Union Labour Force Survey database: http://appsso.eurostat.ec.europa.eu/nui/show.do?dataset=lfsa_ewpshi&lang=en

Foster, R. G., & Kreitzman, L. (2005). *Rhythms of Life: The Biological Clocks That Control the Daily Lives of Every Living Thing.* New Haven: Yale University Press.

Freehling, A. (2007). The Consequences of Living in a 24 Hour Culture. *Newport News Daily Press*, from http://www.dailypress.com/health/dp-hbsummer07-self-cp,0,1288919.story

Gersick, C. J. G. (1988). Time and Transition in Work Teams: Toward a New Model of Group Development. . *Academy of Management Journal, 31*(1), 9-41.

Gopal, A., Espinosa, J. A., Gosain, S., & Darcy, D. P. (2011). Coordination and Performance in Global Software Service Delivery: The Vendor's Perspective. *IEEE Transactions on Engineering Management* (in press).

Grinter, R. E., Herbsleb, J. D., & Perry, D. E. (1999, November). *The Geography of Coordination: Dealing with Distance in R&D Work*. Paper presented at the International ACM SIGGROUP Conference on Supporting Group Work (Group 99 proceedings), Phoenix, Arizona.

Gumm, D. C. (2007). *Mutual Dependency of Distribution, Benefits and Causes: An Empirical Study*. Paper presented at the International Conference on Global Software Engineering (ICGSE proceedings).

Hall, E. (1973). *The Silent Language*: Anchor.

Hancock, P. A., Vercruyssen, M., & Rodenburg, G. J. (1992). The Effect of Gender and Time-of-Day on Time Perception and Mental Workload. *Current Psychology, 11*(3), 203-225.

Hassan, R., & Purser, R. E. (2007). *24/7:Time and Temporality in the Network Society*. Stanford University Press

Heejin, L., & Liebenau, J. (2000). Time and the Internet at the Turn of the Millennium. *Time & Society, 9*(1), 43-56.

Herbsleb, J. D., & Mockus, A. (2003, September 1-9). *Formulation and Preliminary Test of an Empirical Theory of Coordination in Software Engineering*. Paper presented at the European Software Engineering Conference, Symposium on the Foundations of Software Engineering, Helsinki, Finland.

Hindu. (2005, Feb 19). Brand India, a Sum of Different Parts. *The Hindu Business Line*, from http://www.thehindubusinessline.com/2005/02/19/stories/2005021902820400.htm

Holford-Strevens, L. (2005). *The History of Time: A Very Short Introduction* Oxford University Press.

Horne, J., Brass, C., & Pettitt, A. (1980). Circadian Performance. *Ergonomics, 23*(1), 29-36.

ILO. (1990). *Night Work Convention*: International Labour Organisation.

Kotlarsky, J., & Oshri, I. (2005). Social Ties, Knowledge Sharing and Successful Collaboration in Globally Distributed System Development Projects. *European Journal of Information Systems, 14*(1), 37-48.

Kraut, R. E., & Streeter, L. A. (1995). Coordination in Software Development. *Communications of the ACM, 38*(3), 69-81.

Kuper, H., & Marmot, M. (2003). Job Strain, Job Demands, Decision Latitude, and Risk of Coronary Heart Disease within the Whitehall Ii Study. *Epidemiologic Community Health, 57*(2), 147-153.

Lacity, M., Carmel, E., & Rottman, J. (forthcoming 2011). Rural Outsourcing: Buying it Services from Remote Domestic Suppliers. *IEEE Computer*.

Levine, R. V. (1998). *A Geography of Time: On Tempo, Culture, and the Pace of Life*: Basic Books.

Lister, K. (2010). Workshifting Benefits: The Bottom Line. *Telework Research Network*.

Lu, M., Wynn, E., Chudoba, K., & Watson-Manheim, M. (2003). *Understanding Virtuality in a Global Organization: Toward a Virtuality Index*. Paper presented at the 24th International Conference in Information Systems (ICIS proceedings).

Malone, T. (1987). Modeling Coordination in Organizations and Markets. *Management Science 33*(10), 1317-1332.

Mandel, M. (2005, October 3). The Real Reasons You're Working So Hard. *Businessweek*.

March, J., & Simon, H. A. (1958). *Organizations*. New York: John Wiley and Sons.

Mark, G., Gonzalez, V. M., & Harris., J. (2005). *No Task Left Behind?: Examining the Nature of Fragmented Work*. Paper presented at the SIGCHI conference on Human factors in computing systems (CHI '05 proceedings), New York, NY, USA.

References

McMenamin, T. M. (2007). A Time to Work: Recent Trends in Shift Work and Flexible Schedules. *Monthly Lab.*

Mercer. (October 2009). *Employee Statutory and Public Holiday Entitlements – Global Comparisons.* London.

Miller, A. (2009). *Distributed Agile Development: Experiments at Microsoft.* Paper presented at Agile 2009.

Mirchandani, K. (2003). Making Americans: Transnational Call Centre Work in India, University of Waikato, New Zealand.

Monk, T., & Folkard, S. (1992). *Making Shift Work Tolerable:* Taylor and Francis.

Nan, N., Espinosa, J. A., & Carmel, E. (2009). *Communication and Performance across Time Zones: A Laboratory Experiment.* Paper presented at the International Conference on Information Systems, Phoenix, Arizona.

Norgate, S. (2006). *Beyond 9 to 5: Your Life in Time (Maps of the Mind):* Columbia University Press.

O'Leary, M. B., & Cummings, J. N. (2007). The Spatial, Temporal, and Configurational Characteristics of Geographic Dispersion in Teams. *MIS Quarterly, 31*(3).

OPM. (2008). *Status of Telework in the Federal Government:* United States Office of Personnel Management.

Palmer, J. (2011, May 19). Amondawa Tribe Lacks Abstract Idea of Time, Study Says. *BBC.*

Parnas, D. L. (1972). On the Criteria to Be Used in Decomposing Systems into Modules. *Communications of the ACM, 15*(12), 1053-1058.

Peters, T., & Waterman, R. (1988). *In Search of Excellence: Lessons from Americas' Best Run Companies:* Grand Central Publishing.

Richtel, M. (2010, November 21). Growing up Digital, Wired for Distraction. *New York Times.*

Sagi, Y. (2005, April 5). The Night of a New Day. *Ha'aretz.*

Sassen, S. (2000). Spatialities and Temporalities of the Global: Elements for a Theorization. *Public Culture, 12,* 215-232.

Saunders, C., Slyke, C. V., & Vogel, D. R. (2004). My Time or Yours? Managing Time Visions in Global Virtual Teams. *The Academy of Management Executive, 18*(1), 19-31.

Segalla, M. (2010, October). Why Mumbai at 1 PM Is the Center of the Business World. *Harvard Business Review.*

Siebdrat, F., Hoegl, M., & Ernst, H. (2009). How to Manage Virtual Teams. *Sloan Management Review, Summer*(4), 63-68.

Smith, P. G., & Reinertsen, D. G. (1991). *Developing Products in Half the Time.* New York: Van Nostrand Reinhold.

Southerton, D. (2003). "Squeezing Time":Allocating Practices, Coordinating Networks and Scheduling Society. *Time & Society, 12*(1).

Stein, E., & Daude, C. (2007). Longitude Matters: Time Zones and the Location of Foreign Direct Investment. *Journal of International Economics, 71*(1), 96-112.

Tang, J. C., Zhao, C., Cao, X., & Inkpen, K. (2011, March). *Your Time Zone or Mine? A Study of Globally Time Zone-Shifted Collaboration.* Paper presented at the Computer Supported Collaborative Work (CSCW Proceedings).

Teasley, S., Covi, L., Krishnan, M. S., & Olson, J. S. (2000). *How Does Radical Collocation Help a Team Succeed?* Paper presented at the Computer Supported Cooperative Work (CSCW proceedings).

Telegraph. (2009, November 12). Russia Has Too Many Time Zones, Dmitry Medvedev Says *The Daily Telegraph.* Retrieved from http://www.telegraph.co.uk/news/worldnews/europe/russia/6557425/Russia-has-too-many-time-zones-Dmitry-Medvedev-says.html

Thompson, A. (2008, July). Living on Mars Time: Scientists Suffer Perpetual Jet Lag. *Space.com*, from http://www.space.com/5668-living-mars-time-scientists-suffer-perpetual-jet-lag.html

Times-of-India. (2010, January 29). Offshoring Won't Be Impacted. *The Times of India*.

Vijayan, J. (1996). Seven by Twenty-Four. *Computerworld, 30*(9), 102.

Virtanen, M., Ferrie, J. E., Gimeno, D., Vahtera, J., Elovainio, M., Singh-Manoux, A., et al. (2009). Long Working Hours and Sleep Disturbances: The Whitehall Ii Prospective Cohort Study. *Sleep, 32*(6), 737-745.

Westenholz, A. (2006). Identity, Times and Work. *Time & Society, 15*(1), 33-55.

Whitrow, G. J. (1988). *Time in History : The Evolution of Our General Awareness of Time and Temporal Perspective*: Oxford University Press.

Wittenbaum, G. M., & Stasser, G. (1996). Management of Information in Small Groups. In J. L. Nye & A. M. Brower (Eds.), *What's Social About Social Cognition?* (pp. 3-27). Thousand Oaks, California: Sage Publications.

Working Mother. (August 2009). Working Mother 100 Best Companies 2009.

Zerubavel, E. (1985). *Hidden Rhythms: Schedules and Calendars in Social Life*: University of California Press.

Glossary

agile—A software development approach that emphasizes client collaboration, team member interaction, and quick iterations. See chapters 3, 7.

async—Short for asynchronous, meaning not at the same time. See also "sync."

average handle time—A call center metric for the average duration of one transaction of client call. See chapter 6.

bridged—One of the six basic time zone configurations. In this configuration, one liaison bridges/ overlaps distant sites in two time zones. See also "East–West." See chapter 2.

calendar efficiency—The percentage of all of the calendar time that is used productively for work during the 168 hours available per week. See chapter 6.

circadian rhythms—A 24-hour cycle that is synchronized with the light and dark, and is driven by the Earth's rotation. See chapter 8.

concrete time culture—Those cultures that see time as concrete and objective (also known as monochronic). Deadlines are firm and strict. People are punctual to meetings. Germans and Americans tend to be in this group. The opposite of elastic time culture. See chapter 9.

clustered—One of the six basic time zone configurations. In this configuration, members work in various locations and time zones, but there is one central dominant site/time zone where a large percentage of members are located. See chapter 2.

cold spots—The unscheduled time around which family and friends can enjoy themselves. See chapter 8.

co-located—One of the six basic time zone configurations, in which all team members reside at the same location. See chapter 2.

conventional global approaches—Parallel or phase-based, as opposed to the "Follow-the-Sun" approach. See chapter 6.

coordination mix—The portfolio of coordination tactics that are adopted and used by collaborators. See also "coordination tactic." See chapter 10.

conveyance processes—The transmission of new information to enable the receiver to *create* and *revise* a mental model of the situation. See chapter 10.

coordination tactic—A mechanism or process used by collaborators. There are three types:

mechanistic (based on processes and routines), organic (based on communication), and implicit (based on collaborators' knowledge). See also "coordination mix." See chapter 10.

coordination—The management of dependencies among task activities. Alternative definition: the act of integrating each task and organizational unit so that it contributes to the overall objective. See chapter 10.

convergence—Collaborators across time zones coming together, to create, to agree, to build the same "mental model" in their heads and resolve any miscommunication. See chapter 3.

convergence window—The overlap time window between individuals and sites, across time zones, which is used for converging, typically by voice, on work issues. See chapter 3.

distraction science—A new specialty discipline about how people focus on tasks and get distracted from tasks. See chapter 9.

distributed work—Work by teams and/or individuals who are not at the same location. See chapter 1.

DST—Daylight Saving Time. A region moves the clock forward during summer. DST narrows/ widens time separation with locations that do not have DST. See chapter 1.

elastic time culture—Also known as polychronic. The cultures in which deadlines are flexible; includes Latinos, the French (to some extent), and Indians. The opposite of concrete time culture. See chapter 9.

e-mail chain—Refers to a sequence of unresolved e-mails sent between distributed team members seeking clarification. See chapter 1.

escalation process— Raising work issues to higher authorities for urgent resolution. See chapter 3.

external interruptions—Situations when someone or something makes us stop the work we are doing. See chapter 4.

far-flung—One of the six basic time zone configurations. In this configuration, individuals are widely scattered across various locations and time zones. See chapter 2.

fixed shift—A work schedule that remains the same from day to day. See chapter 3.

flexitime—Employees work on flexible schedules. See chapter 3.

Follow-the-Sun—A type of global workflow strategy in which unfinished work is handed-off from one site to another site to the west. The business goal is speed, while Round-the-Clock is about 24-hour coverage. See chapter 6.

GMT—Greenwich Mean Time.

granular—Small size tasks that can be handled quickly; for example, helpdesk tasks, which may be handled in a few minutes. For granular work, there is little coordination challenge in handing-off work between various global sites since the sites do not hand-off much half-finished work.

Gregorian calendar—Also known as the Western calendar, or Christian calendar, is the internationally accepted civil calendar.

handoff—The handoff transfers and resolves the essential information for all unfinished work. We recommend that the handoff have both written and verbal components. See chapter 3.

horarium—The schedule used by the medieval Benedictine monasteries of Europe. It is one of the earliest forms of societal rhythm of time. See chapter 9.

hot spots—Scheduled commitments such as work, sleep, chores. See chapter 8.

implicit coordination—The coordination based on unspoken assumptions about what others are likely to do; achieved from knowledge team members have about each other and about the task activities of others in the team. See chapter 10.

internal interruptions—The situations in which we stop the work we are doing with no apparent external cause. See chapter 9.

Internet Time—A time standard with no time zones, measured in beats. It was introduced by Swatch, the watch company, in 1998. See Prologue.

irregular shift—A work schedule that is variable and erratic. See chapter 3.

job strain model—A concept that measures two main components of stress: high job demands (the need to work quickly and hard) and low decision latitude (which includes time allocation). See chapter 8.

knowledge worker—An educated professional that acts on and communicates with knowledge within a specific subject area. Knowledge workers include programmers, managers, teachers, designers, doctors, and lawyers.

liaison—See "temporal liaison."

MBTA—Management By Timeshifting Around. Managers stay in place but timeshift to different locations by adjusting or scattering their workdays. See chapter 3.

MBWA—Management By Wandering Around. See chapter 3.

microsourcing—One of the global sourcing models where buyers source small projects or fractional tasks. Similar to crowdsourcing. See chapter 6.

multitasking—Refers to knowledge workers performing more than one task at the same time. See chapter 9.

nearshoring—Sourcing service work to a foreign, lower-wage country that is relatively close in distance or time zone (or both). See chapter 5.

night work—Any work that directly touches the span from 00:00 to 05:00. See chapters 3, 8.

nomadism—The subculture of working anywhere. Many nomads work in cafés, in "third places," not their home or office. See chapter 1.

organic coordination—Individuals communicate naturally, often unscheduled, in order to coordinate and problem-solve. This is one of three coordination tactics. See also "coordination tactics." See chapter 10.

overlap window—A period of time when distributed teams overlap their work hours. See also "convergence window." See chapter 3.

Phalanx—IBM's original Follow-the-Sun structure. See chapter 6.

production support—A common type of global IT work for supporting the IT systems/applications in organizations, often including some kind of technical call center. See chapter 1.

quiet time—Uninterrupted time that is the result of reduced interruptions during the workday, which in turn is due to scattered project team work. See chapter 9.

radical co-location—A very tight seating arrangement that we now commonly see in agile team-rooms. Designed to encourage constant sharing of knowledge. See chapter 9.

radical timeshifting—Akin to working the graveyard/night shift in traditional shifts of factories and hospitals. See chapter 3.

rapid prototyping—Very quick construction of a demo. This is an example of a task that can be done using Follow-the-Sun. It is a creative, constructive task with serious coordination challenges. See chapter 6.

rotating shift—A work schedule designed for hours that change regularly as, for example, from day shift to evening shift to night shift. Rotation may be rapid (e.g., within three days), mid-length (e.g., one week) or long (e.g., four weeks) and rotate forward or backward. See chapter 3.

Round-the-Clock—A type of global workflow strategy that leverages time zones to achieve 24-hour coverage. The business goal is 24-hour coverage, while Follow-the-Sun is focused on speed. See chapter 6.

Rule of Two—An informal rule where the number of sites collaborating on the same project at the same time is intentionally limited to two. See chapter 5.

scattertime—A relatively new mode of work where knowledge workers spread out their labor into scattered chunks of time, broken up by home and personal time. See chapter 1.

schedule—The artifact that is the rhythm we all live by, like a metronome in our lives.

SHIFt—An acronym for the four basic parameters for timeshifting: Standardized, How long, number of Individual participants, Frequency. See chapter 3.

shiftwork—Any nonstandard work schedule designed for work hours that stretch beyond the typical daylight periods of 07:00 to 18:00. See chapter 3.

site location—Or site selection. A distributed organization design factor. See chapter 5.

sync—Short for synchronous, meaning at the same time. See also "async."

task delay—A delay in completing a task. Time zone separation breaks the rhythm of synchronous interaction and workflow, thus leading to delay, whereas mere spatial distance removes the benefits of co-presence but members can still work synchronously when needed. See chapter 10.

telework—Working from home. See chapter 3.

temporal—Relating to time.

temporal liaison—A person who bridges time zones by timeshifting, usually every day. See chapter 3.

temporal regularity—A phenomenon that involves the structuring of social life by forcing activities into fairly rigid temporal patterns. See chapter 9.

Tier 1 support—A type of IT support services, similar to helpdesk, often for more technical queries. See chapter 6.

time colonialism—Capitalism allows the wealthy to colonize the workers of developing countries into the time zones of the wealthy. See Epilogue.

time liaison—See "temporal liaison."

time management—The act or process of exercising conscious control over the amount of time spent on specific activities, especially to increase efficiency or productivity. See chapter 9.

time perception—Certain objective units of time are perceived differently by different people. See chapter 9.

time sovereignty—Control over your own work schedule. See chapter 1.

time zone pain—A website developed by IBM that tries to minimize the collective pain of finding a meeting window that is least disruptive. See chapter 1.

time zone robustness (TZR)—A model with four levels that describes and prescribes deliberate actions around time zone-driven collaboration. The four levels of robustness range from least deliberate to reactive to strategically-driven. See chapter 4.

time zone strategy matrix—Captures the intersection of time zones and the nature of the work in a two-dimensional matrix. See the introduction to Section II and chapter 5.

time-boxing—The setting of strict deadlines in each work iteration. Used in software. See chapter 6.

timeshifting—Moving your work hours to accommodate someone else's work hours in order to synchronize and converge. See chapter 3.

time-to-market—The length of time it takes from product conception until the product is available for use or sale. See chapter 6.

UTC—Coordinated Universal Time. See also "GMT."

waterfall—A sequential software development model in which progress is seen as flowing steadily downwards (like a waterfall) through the phases of conception, initiation, analysis, design, construction, testing, production/implementation, and maintenance. See chapter 4.

zoner—Experienced, multi-time zone worker. See chapter 1.

Zulu—Military standard time; uses GMT. See Prologue.

CPSIA information can be obtained at www.ICGtesting.com
Printed in the USA
LVOW032009030112

262236LV00006B/97/P

9 780983 992509